ONTARIO NATURE GUIDE

Krista Kagume

with contributions from

Andy Bezener & Linda Kershaw

Lone Pine Publishing

Co-published by Partners Publishing and Lone Pine Media Productions (B.C.) Ltd.

Distributed by: Canada Book Distributors - Booklogic
11414-119 Street
Edmonton, AB   T5G 2X6   Canada
Tel: 1-800-661-9017

Library and Archives Canada Cataloguing in Publication

Kagume, Krista
     Ontario nature guide / Krista Kagume.

Reprint. Originally published: Edmonton : Lone Pine Pub., 2008.
Co-published by: Lone Pine Media Productions (B.C.) Ltd.
Includes bibliographical references and index.
ISBN 978-1-77213-036-2 (paperback), 978-1-77213-037-9 (e-pub)

1. Natural history—Ontario—Guidebooks. I. Title.
QH106.2.O5K33 2008   578.09713   C2016-907423-5

Editorial Director: Nancy Foulds
Project Editor: Nicholle Carrière
Editorial: Genevieve Boyer, Kathy van Denderen, Volker Bodegom, Nicholle Carrière
Illustration Coordinator: Carol Woo
Production Manager: Gene Longson
Book Design: Heather Markham
Layout and Production: Michael Cooke, Trina Koscielnuk, Megan Fischer, Volker Bodegom
Cover Design: Gerry Dotto
Cover Illustrations: Linda Dunn, Ted Nordhagen, Gary Ross, Ian Sheldon
Illustrations: please see p. 4 for a complete list of credits

Disclaimer: This guide is not intended to be a "how to" reference guide for food or medicinal uses of plants. We do not recommend experimentation by readers, and we caution that a number of woody plants in Ontario, including some used traditionally as medicines, are poisonous and harmful.

We acknowledge the financial support of the Government of Canada.

Funded by the Government of Canada
Financé par le gouvernement du Canada | Canada

PC: 28

TABLE OF CONTENTS

ILLUSTRATION CREDITS

Frank Burman: 147b, 149c, 160a, 160b, 161a, 161d, 162a, 162b, 162c, 163a, 163d, 164c, 164d, 164e, 164f, 165c, 166, 167a, 167c, 168, 171b, 171c, 174b, 174c, 175, 176a, 176c, 177b, 177c, 178, 179a, 180, 185a, 185b, 186a, 186b, 187b, 188a, 191c, 192a, 194a, 194c, 195, 196, 197

Ivan Droujinin: 131b, 132, 138

Linda Dunn: 174a, 176b, 188b

Kindrie Grove: 52b, 58a, 67c

Ted Nordhagen: 73b, 74a, 81c, 82b, 86b, 89b, 90b, 92, 93, 95b, 95c, 97a, 97b, 98b, 99, 100, 101b, 102a, 102b, 103a, 104b, 105a, 105b, 106a, 106b, 107, 108

George Penetrante: 122c, 123a, 123c, 124b, 127b, 127c, 128a, 128b, 129

Ewa Pluciennik: 91a

Gary Ross: 44, 45, 46, 47, 48, 49, 50, 51, 52a, 53, 54, 55, 56, 57, 58b, 58c, 59, 60, 61, 62, 63, 64, 65, 66, 67a, 67b, 68, 69, 72, 73a, 74b, 75, 76, 77, 78, 79, 80, 81a, 81b, 82a, 83, 84, 85, 86a, 86c, 87, 88, 89a, 89c, 90a, 90c, 91b, 94, 95a, 96, 97c, 98a, 98c, 101a, 101c, 102c, 103b, 103c, 104a, 104c, 105c, 106c, 110, 111, 112, 113, 114, 115, 116, 117, 118, 119

Ian Sheldon: 42, 43, 122a, 122b, 123b, 124a, 124c, 125, 126, 127a, 128c, 131a, 131c, 133, 134, 135, 136, 137, 142, 143, 144, 145, 146, 147a, 147c, 148, 149a, 149b, 150, 151, 152, 153a, 154, 155, 156, 157, 160c, 161b, 161c, 162d, 162e, 163b, 163c, 164a, 164b, 165a, 165b, 165d, 165e, 167b, 169, 170a, 170b, 170c, 177a, 177d, 179b, 179c, 181, 182, 183, 184, 185c, 185d, 186c, 187a, 187c, 188c, 189, 190, 191a, 191b, 192b, 192c, 193, 194b, 194d

ACKNOWLEDGMENTS

Thank you to Erling Holm, Antonia Guidotti and their colleagues at the Royal Ontario Museum for their advice on Ontario's fish and insects, and to botanists Vicky Filion and Gisèle Mitrow for suggestions on which plants to include. Thanks to Andy Bezener and Linda Kershaw for their work on the first of this nature guide series, the *Rocky Mountain Nature Guide*.

MAMMALS

Beluga
p. 42

Walrus
p. 42

Ringed Seal
p. 43

Bearded Seal
p. 43

North American Elk
p. 44

White-tailed Deer
p. 44

Moose
p. 45

Caribou
p. 45

Cougar
p. 46

Canada Lynx
p. 46

Bobcat
p. 47

Striped Skunk
p. 47

American Marten
p. 48

Fisher
p. 48

Short-tailed Weasel
p. 49

Long-tailed Weasel
p. 49

Mink
p. 49

Wolverine
p. 50

Badger
p. 50

Northern River Otter
p. 51

Raccoon
p. 51

Black Bear
p. 52

Polar Bear
p. 52

Coyote
p. 53

MAMMALS

Grey Wolf
p. 53

Arctic Fox
p. 54

Red Fox
p. 54

Grey Fox
p. 55

Porcupine
p. 55

Meadow Jumping Mouse
p. 56

Woodland Jumping
p. 56

Norway Rat
p. 56

House Mouse
p. 57

Deer Mouse
p. 57

White-footed Mouse
p. 57

Southern Red-backed Vole
p. 58

Meadow Vole
p. 58

Southern Bog Lemming
p. 58

Muskrat
p. 59

Beaver
p. 59

Eastern Chipmunk
p. 60

Least Chipmunk
p. 60

Woodchuck
p. 60

Red Squirrel
p. 61

Eastern Grey Squirrel
p. 61

Northern Flying Squirrel
p. 61

Southern Flying Squirrel
p. 62

European Hare
p. 62

7

MAMMALS

Snowshoe
p. 63

Eastern Cottontail
p. 63

Northern Bat
p. 64

Little Brown Bat
p. 64

Eastern Small-footed Bat
p. 64

Eastern Red Bat
p. 65

Hoary Bat
p. 65

Silver-haired Bat
p. 65

Big Brown Bat
p. 66

Eastern Pipistrelle
p. 66

Hairy-tailed Mole
p. 67

Star-nosed Mole
p. 67

Masked Shrew
p. 67

Common Water Shrew
p. 68

Pygmy Shrew
p. 68

Northern Short-tailed
Shrew, p. 68

Virginia Opossum
p. 69

BIRDS

Canada Goose
p. 72

Tundra Swan
p. 72

Mallard
p. 73

Blue-winged Teal
p. 73

Black Scoter
p. 74

Bufflehead
p. 74

Common Goldeneye
p. 75

Common Merganser
p. 75

Ruffed Grouse
p. 76

Spruce Grouse
p. 76

Common Loon
p. 77

Pied-billed Grebe
p. 77

Double-crested Cormorant
p. 77

Great Blue Heron
p. 78

Green Heron
p. 78

Black-crowned Night-heron
p. 79

Turkey Vulture
p. 79

Osprey
p. 80

Bald Eagle
p. 80

Northern Harrier
p. 80

Broad-winged Hawk
p. 81

Red-tailed Hawk
p. 81

American Kestrel
p. 81

Sandhill Crane
p. 82

Killdeer
p. 82

Spotted Sandpiper
p. 83

Greater Yellowlegs
p. 83

Wilson's Snipe
p. 83

Bonaparte's Gull
p. 84

Ring-billed Gull
p. 84

Herring Gull
p. 84

Black Tern
p. 85

9

Common Tern
p. 85

Rock Pigeon
p. 86

Mourning Dove
p. 86

Black-billed Cuckoo
p. 86

Eastern Screech-Owl
p. 87

Great Horned Owl
p. 87

Snowy Owl
p. 87

Northern Saw-whet Owl
p. 88

Common Highthawk
p. 88

Whip-poor-will
p. 88

Chimney Swift
p. 89

Ruby-throated Hummingbird
p. 89

Belted Kingfisher
p. 89

Red-headed Woodpecker
p. 90

Yellow-bellied Sapsucker
p. 90

Downy Woodpecker
p. 90

Northern Flicker
p. 91

Pileated Woodpecker
p. 91

Olive-sided Flycatcher
p. 92

Eastern Phoebe
p. 92

Great Crested Flycatcher
p. 92

Eastern Kingbird
p. 93

Northern Shrike
p. 93

Red-eyed Vireo
p. 93

BIRDS

Gray Jay
p. 94

Blue Jay
p. 94

American Crow
p. 94

Common Raven
p. 95

Horned Lark
p. 95

Purple Martin
p. 95

Tree Swallow
p. 96

Barn Swallow
p. 96

Black-capped Chickadee
p. 96

Red-breasted Nuthatch
p. 97

White-breasted Nuthatch
p. 97

House Wren
p. 97

Marsh Wren
p. 98

Ruby-crowned Kinglet
p. 98

Eastern Bluebird
p. 98

Hermit Thrush
p. 99

American Robin
p. 99

Gray Catbird
p. 99

Brown Thrasher
p. 100

European Starling
p. 100

Cedar Waxwing
p. 100

Yellow Warbler
p. 101

Yellow-rumped Warbler
p. 101

American Redstart
p. 101

Ovenbird
p. 102

Common Yellowthroat
p. 102

Scarlet Tanager
p. 102

Chipping Sparrow
p. 103

Song Sparrow
p. 103

White-throated Sparrow
p. 103

Dark-eyed Junco
p. 104

Northern Cardinal
p. 104

Rose-breasted Grosbeak
p. 104

Indigo Bunting
p. 105

Bobolink
p. 105

Red-winged Blackbird
p. 105

Eastern Meadowlark
p. 106

Brown-headed cowbird
p. 106

Baltimore Oriole
p. 106

Purple Finch
p. 107

Common Redpoll
p. 107

American Goldfinch
p. 108

House Sparrow
p. 108

Mudpuppy
p. 110

Eastern Newt
p. 110

Spotted Salamander
p. 110

Northern Two-lined
Salamander, p. 111

Four-toed Salamander
p. 111

Eastern Red-backed
Salamander, p. 111

American Toad
p. 112

Gray Treefrog
p. 112

Spring Peeper
p. 112

Western Chorus Frog
p. 113

American Bullfrog
p. 113

Green Frog
p. 113

Northern Leopard Frog
p. 114

Mink Frog
p. 114

Wood Frog
p. 114

Common Snapping Turtle
p. 115

Stinkpot
p. 115

Spiny Softshell Turtle
p. 115

Painted Turtle
p. 116

Blanding's Turtle
p. 116

Northern Map Turtle
p. 116

Common Five-lined Skink
p. 117

Common Gartersnake
p. 117

DeKay's Brownsnake
p. 117

AMPHIBIANS & REPTILES

Red-bellied Snake
p. 118

Smooth Greensnake
p. 118

Ring-necked Snake
p. 118

Northern Watersnake
p. 119

Milk Snake
p. 119

Massasauga
p. 119

FISH

Sea Lamprey
p. 122

Lake Sturgeon
p. 122

Common Carp
p. 122

Emerald Shiner
p. 123

White Sucker
p. 123

Channel Catfish
p. 123

Northern Pike
p. 124

Rainbow Smelt
p. 124

Chinook Salmon
p. 124

Rainbow Trout
p. 125

Brown Trout
p. 125

Brook Trout
p. 125

Lake Trout
p. 126

Lake Whitefish
p. 126

Burbot
p. 126

Brook Stickleback
p. 127

Mottled Sculpin
p. 127

Smallmouth Bass
p. 127

White Bass
p. 128

Pumpkinseed
p. 128

Walleye
p. 128

Freshwater Drum
p. 129

American Eel
p. 129

Round Goby
p. 129

Caddisfly
p. 131

Zebra Mussel
p. 131

Mayfly
p. 131

Virile Crayfish
p. 132

Water Strider
p. 132

Grovesnail
p. 132

Cabbage White
p. 133

Eastern Tiger Swallowtail
p. 133

INVERTEBRATES

Spring Azure
p. 133

Mourning Cloak
p. 134

Monarch
p. 134

Luna Moth
p. 134

Common Green Darner
p. 135

Firefly
p. 135

Multicoloured Asian Ladybug
p. 135

Dog-day Cicada
p. 136

Mosquitoes
p. 136

Carpenter Ant
p. 136

Yellow Jackets
p. 137

Bumble Bee
p. 137

Harvestmen
p. 137

Banded Garden Spider
p. 138

Dark Fishing Spider
p. 138

House Centipede
p. 138

TREES

Balsam Fir
p. 142

White Spruce
p. 142

Black Spruce
p. 143

Tamarack
p. 143

Eastern Hemlock
p. 144

Eastern White Pine
p. 144

Red Pine
p. 145

Jack Pine
p. 145

Eastern White-Cedar
p. 146

White Elm
p. 146

Butternut
p. 147

Bitternut Hickory
p. 147

American Beech
p. 148

Bur Oak
p. 148

Red Oak
p. 149

Ironwood
p. 149

Yellow Birch
p. 150

Paper Birch
p. 150

Large-toothed Aspen
p. 151

Trembling Aspen
p. 151

Balsam Poplar
p. 152

Pin Cherry
p. 152

American Mountain-ash
p. 153

Hawthorns
p. 153

Staghorn Sumac
p. 154

American Basswood
p. 154

Eastern Flowering Dogwood
p. 155

Sugar Maple
p. 155

Silver Maple
p. 156

Red Maple
p. 156

Mountain Maple
p. 157

Striped Maple
p. 157

White Ash
p. 157

SHRUBS

Canada Yew
p. 160

Crowberry
p. 160

Common Juniper
p. 160

Sand Heather
p. 161

Green Alder
p. 161

Dwarf Birch
p. 161

Beaked Hazelnut
p. 162

Willows
p.162

Buffaloberry
p. 162

Alder-leaved Buckthorn
p. 163

Red-osier Dogwood
p. 163

Narrow-leaved Meadowsweet
p. 163

Red-twigged Serviceberry
p. 164

Cloudberry
p. 164

Wild Red Raspberry
p. 164

Prickly Wild Rose
p. 165

Three-toothed Cinquefoil
p. 165

Bristly Black Currant
p. 165

Skunk Currant
p. 166

Lingonberry
p. 166

Velvet Leaf Blueberry
p. 166

Dwarf Blueberry
p. 167

Bearberry
p. 167

SHRUBS

Trailing Arbutus
p. 167

Leatherleaf
p. 168

Bog Rosemary
p. 168

Labrador Tea
p. 168

Prince's-pine
p. 169

Twinflower
p. 169

Bracted Honeysuckle
p. 169

Common Snowberry
p. 170

Nannyberry
p. 170

Highbush Cranberry
p. 170

Common Elderberry
p. 171

Poison Ivy
p. 171

HERBS, GRASSES & FERNS

Yellow Pond-lily
p. 174

White Water-lily
p. 174

Skunk Cabbage
p. 174

Jack-in-the-pulpit
p. 175

Pitcher-plant
p. 175

Common Bladderwort
p. 175

Sundew
p. 176

Wood Lily
p. 176

White Trillium
p. 176

White Death-camas
p. 177

Wild Lily-of-the-valley
p. 177

Star-flowered Solomon's-seal
p. 177

HERBS, GRASSES & FERNS

Northern Blue Flag
p. 178

Common Blue-eyed-grass
p. 178

Yellow Lady's-slipper
p. 178

Tall Meadowrue
p. 178

Red Baneberry
p. 179

Meadow Buttercup
p. 179

Yellow Marsh-marigold
p. 180

Canada Anemone
p. 180

Common Silverweed
p. 180

Wild Strawberry
p. 181

Bunchberry
p. 181

American Vetch
p. 181

Bigleaf Lupine
p. 182

Alfalfa
p. 182

Sweet-clover
p. 182

Alsike Clover
p. 183

Red Clover
p. 183

Early Blue Violet
p. 183

Cultivated Flax
p. 184

Harebell
p. 184

Spreading Dogbane
p. 184

Common Milkweed
p. 185

Purple Loosestrife
p. 185

Common Fireweed
p. 185

Common Evening-primrose
p. 186

Common St. John's-wort
p. 186

Great Mullein
p. 186

Butter-and-eggs
p. 187

Spotted Touch-me-not
p. 187

Common Pink Wintergreen
p. 187

Stinging Nettle
p. 188

Wild Bergamot
p. 188

Wild Purple Teasel
p. 188

Spotted Knapweed
p. 189

Canada Thistle
p. 189

Bull Thistle
p. 189

Chicory
p. 190

Common Dandelion
p. 190

Yellow Hawkweed
p. 190

Perennial Sow-thistle
p. 191

Oxeye Daisy
p. 191

Black-eyed Susan
p. 191

Fringed Aster
p. 192

Pineapple-weed
p. 192

Common Tansy
p. 192

Canada Goldenrod
p. 193

Pearly Everlasting
p. 193

Common Yarrow
p. 193

HERBS, GRASSES & FERNS

Spotted Water-hemlock
p. 194

Common Cow-parsnip
p. 194

Northern Bedstraw
p. 194

Curly Dock
p. 195

Common Plantain
p. 195

English Plantain
p. 195

Common Reed Grass
p. 196

Wild Rice
p. 196

Common Cattail
p. 196

Bracken Fern
p. 197

Ostrich Fern
p. 197

Common Horsetail
p. 197

Those who have lived in or travelled through Ontario will never forget the incredible beauty and rich diversity of life found here. Renowned for stunning autumn colours, rocky ridges, sandy beaches and abundant lakes, Ontario is home to one-quarter of the world's fresh water. The province provides us with unique, accessible wildness and spectacular landscape features that hold a secret magic. When you visit Ontario's natural areas, it will become apparent to you how the plants and animals are integral components of this ecosystem.

Many of us are thrilled by the sight of brilliant summer wildflowers and lush green trees, vivid butterflies, fish, reptiles and amphibians, colourful birds and curious mammals. By learning to identify the species and their various roles in the province's ecosystem, our Ontario experience becomes much more rewarding. This guide is for people who have found beauty and wonder in Ontario's natural areas and have longed to understand more about its wild inhabitants. We hope this guide will enhance your encounters with the plants and animals of the province, inspire you to understand their importance, and allow you to discover first-hand the true joy and wonder of Ontario.

ONTARIO'S ECOREGIONS

The natural regions of Ontario are extremely diverse. This province, the second largest in Canada, represents a little more than 10% of Canada's land area, and it encompasses a dramatic variety of landscapes. Extensive boreal forests, clear blue lakes, major rivers, diverse deciduous forests, expansive tundra and icy coastal waters all contribute to the scenic beauty and ecological uniqueness of this region. Ontario stretches 1685 km from its northernmost point on Hudson Bay to its southernmost point, Pelee Island. Its east-to-west extent is more than 1628 km, giving it an overall area of 1,068,580 km². As much as 75% of Ontario is forested, and almost 17% is inland water.

The wildlife and wildlife associations that occur in Ontario are linked to the geological, climatic and biological influences of its varied biogeography. For simplification, this book divides the province into 5 natural regions: Tundra, Taiga, Boreal Forest, Mixed Forest and Carolinian Forest. Looking at these regions in detail can lead to a better understanding of how Ontario's animals and plants are linked to their environment.

Tundra

The permafrost belt along the Hudson Bay coast in northern Ontario largely defines the Tundra ecoregion. A permafrost zone indicates land that has a subsurface layer of soil that is frozen all year, regardless of snow cover or season. Geologically, the Tundra zone is part of the Hudson Bay Lowlands, and it is composed primarily of sedimentary rock such as limestone. The few trees that can grow in this ecoregion are small and stunted. Mosses, lichens and low shrubs such as willows, Labrador tea, cranberry, blueberry and crowberry make up the bulk of the vegetation, but animal life is still abundant. The cold, food-rich waters of Hudson Bay support large numbers of fish, which in turn support numerous marine mammals and sea birds. Diverse populations of birds nest in the Tundra, from large tundra swans to smaller sandpipers and redpolls. Human habitation in this region is limited to trading villages near the mouths of major rivers. The animals of this region include the polar bear, caribou, arctic fox, wolverine, arctic shrew, tundra swan, snowy owl, sandhill crane, lake sturgeon and wood frog.

Ecoregions of Ontario

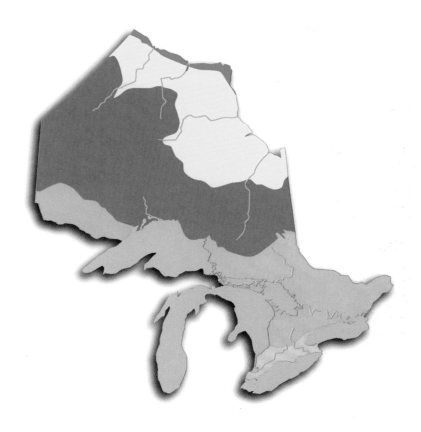

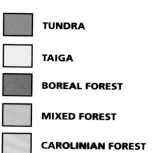

TUNDRA

TAIGA

BOREAL FOREST

MIXED FOREST

CAROLINIAN FOREST

Taiga

The Taiga, also called the Hudson Bay Lowland Forest, is geologically a part of the Canadian Shield (specifically the Laurentian Lowlands). The underlying igneous rock is mainly granite, and its origin is Precambrian. The result is flat, poorly drained land that supports extensive swamps, bogs and patterned fens. The typical vegetation is black spruce and larch in the muskeg zones. Higher and slightly warmer areas can support some deciduous trees such as balsam poplar, trembling aspen and paper birch. Near the edge of James Bay, black spruce is replaced by white spruce, a species better adapted to seashore environments. The Taiga is characterized by long, harsh winters and short, mild summers. Animals common to the Taiga forest include the moose, black bear, grey wolf, American marten, northern bog lemming, hoary bat, northern shrike, common raven, song sparrow, lake trout and northern pike.

Boreal Forest

The famous Boreal Forest is the largest natural region in Ontario and the largest forest region in Canada. Geologically, it is also part of the Canadian Shield. The Boreal Forest is very similar to the more northerly Taiga forest, except that its climate is somewhat milder and it is slightly more diverse biologically. Still, snow is present for 8 or 9 months of the year, and summer temperatures rarely rise above 25°C. The main tree species in the Boreal Forest are black spruce, white spruce, larch, jack pine (in well-drained areas) and balsam fir, but some broad-leaved trees such as paper birch, trembling aspen and balsam poplar also occur. The pristine lakes and rivers add to the scenic beauty of the Boreal Forest, and tourism here is a year-round interest. This region is also mined for its minerals, including copper, zinc, lead, nickel and uranium. A variety of mammals inhabit the Boreal Forest, including the moose, white-tailed deer, black bear, fisher, Canada lynx, snowshoe hare, least weasel, red squirrel, beaver, southern red-backed vole and little brown bat. Many songbirds migrate to the Boreal Forest to nest, including the common loon, osprey, warblers, thrushes, flycatchers and sparrows, whereas other birds such as woodpeckers and chickadees remain year round. Amphibians, reptiles and fish include the common gartersnake, wood frog, American toad, northern leopard frog, lake whitefish, white sucker, burbot and emerald shiner.

Mixed Forest

South of the Boreal Forest is the Mixed Forest, a transitional region of both coniferous and deciduous trees that is also called the Great Lakes–St. Lawrence Forest.
Geologically, this region is at the southern edge of the Canadian Shield
and the St. Lawrence Lowlands. The
complex vegetation of the
Mixed Forest is a mosaic of
eastern white pine, red pine,
eastern hemlock and eastern
white-cedar. Also found here are more
boreal trees species such as spruce, jack pine, larch,
balsam fir, trembling aspen and paper birch, as well as southern deciduous trees
such as yellow birch, red maple, red oak and American beech. The rich forest floor
supports a wide variety of colourful wildflowers, including white trillium, false Solomon's-seal, twinflower and baneberry. The diversity of
vegetation here supports numerous large and small mammals
and birds, including the coyote, bobcat, northern river otter,
long-tailed weasel, porcupine, woodchuck, northern bat,
ruffed grouse, northern flicker, spotted sandpiper and purple
finch. Amphibians and reptiles such as the eastern newt,
mudpuppy, American bullfrog and green frog dwell in
the lakes, ponds and leaf litter. The water bodies of
the Mixed Forest support snapping turtles, northern
pike, rainbow trout, pumpkinseeds and other aquatic
life, while the Great Lakes support abundant, diverse populations
ranging from native mottled sculpin and lake trout to the charis-
matic American eel and more troublesome, introduced round goby,
smelt and zebra mussel.

Carolinian Forest

The Carolinian Forest, also called the Eastern Deciduous Forest, is widespread in the eastern United States but is only found in Canada in the southernmost regions of Ontario. The winters here are mild and relatively short, creating a much longer growing season than elsewhere in the province. Geologically, the Carolinian Forest is part of the Great Lakes and St. Lawrence Lowlands, and sedimentary deposits lie below the rich, deep soils typical of this region. The dominant forest trees here are broad-leaved species such as sugar maple, American beech, American basswood, red ash, white oak and butternut. A few species that thrive here, such as several hickory species, pawpaw, tulip tree, sassafras and Kentucky coffeetree, are found nowhere else in Ontario. Unfortunately, most of the natural forests in this region have been cleared to make way for extensive human settlement, industry and agriculture. The Carolinian Forest is home to many animals, including the white-tailed deer, badger, raccoon, eastern grey squirrel, eastern cottontail, Virginia opossum, wood thrush, pileated woodpecker and ovenbird. Many of our snakes, turtles and other reptiles and amphibians are found here. While a few of these species such as the raccoon, white-tailed deer, American crow and gulls have adapted to human habitation, some, such as the Acadian flycatcher, hooded warbler, queen snake, racer and massasauga, are now found only where pockets of the original forest remain.

HUMAN-ALTERED LANDSCAPES

The impact of human activity on natural environments is visible throughout Ontario, but it is most noticeable in the south. Cities, roadways, agriculture, forestry and mining are just a few examples of the impact we have had on the land. Many of the most common plants and animals that are found in these altered landscapes did not occur here before modern human habitation and transportation. The house mouse, Norway rat, European hare, rock pigeon and house sparrow are some of the highly successful exotic animals that were introduced to North America from Europe and Asia. Chinook salmon, trout and other sport fish have been stocked in our lakes, while smelt and goby found their way in through the ballast water of ships. Some introduced plants, such as purple loosestrife, alfalfa and clover have become troublesome weeds, while others are grown as ornamentals, beautifying our gardens and parks. The distributions of many native plants and animals have changed because of habitat degradation and fragmentation.

THE SEASONS

The seasons of Ontario greatly influence the lives of animals and plants. Birds, bats, marine mammals, fish and some insects migrate, while many other species are confined to relatively slow forms of terrestrial travel. As a result, they have limited geographic ranges and must cope in various ways with the changing seasons.

Spring

The rising temperatures, melting snow and warm rains of spring bring renewal. From woodlands to wetlands, nature comes alive with mating songs and spring activity. Millions of birds pass over the province on their way to northern breeding grounds, while bears and other hibernating creatures awaken and emerge from their long winter slumber. The croaking of mating frogs and toads can be heard in marshes, sloughs and ditches. Longer days of sunshine bring forth the buds of trees and shrubs, and colourful spring wildflowers bloom. Spring brings an abundance of food throughout the food chain: lush new growth provides ample food for herbivores, and the numerous herbivore young become easy prey for the carnivores.

Many animals bear their young at this time of year, though some birds, such as phalaropes and house sparrows, may mate every few months throughout the summer, and others, such as voles and mice, may mate throughout the year. While some small animals, including rodents, amphibians, reptiles, fish and some birds mature within weeks, offspring of the larger mammals and certain birds are dependent on their parents for much longer periods.

Summer

Warmer, longer days of sunshine bring forth wildflower blooms, pupating insect larvae, hawking
birds and newborn animals. Trails, roads, lakes,
streams, campgrounds and townsites suddenly swell
with both wildlife and people. During the warmest time
of the year, forests green and come alive with activity.
Animals' bodies have recovered from the strain of migration, the previous winter's food scarcity and spring's reproductive efforts, but summer is not a time of relaxation. To
prepare for the upcoming winter, some animals must eat large
amounts of energy-rich foods to build up fat reserves, while others work furiously to stockpile food caches in safe places.

Autumn

Ontario is well known for the colourful splendour of its autumn foliage. Maple
leaves turn brilliant red, while trembling aspen and larch brighten forests with
intense bursts of yellow. Autumn is the time when certain bats and birds, as well
other species such as the monarch butterfly, migrate out of the province. Reptiles
and amphibians burrow into the leaf litter,
some mammals prepare their winter
dens and some insects deposit their
eggs in protected places, to hatch
the following spring. For animals such as the large
ungulates, autumn is
the time for mating.

Winter

Winter differs in intensity and duration throughout the different regions of the province. In southern areas, winters are mild and not too stressful. In the northern regions, however, winter can be an arduous, life-threatening challenge for the many mammals and birds that do not migrate southward. For herbivores, high-energy foods are difficult to find, often requiring more energy to locate than they provide in return. Their negative energy budget gradually weakens most herbivores through winter, and those not sufficiently fit at the onset of the cold season end up feeding the equally needy carnivores, which ironically find an ally in winter's severity. Voles and mice also find advantages in the season—an insulating layer of snow buffers their elaborate trails from the worst of winter's cold. Food, shelter and warmth are all found in this thin layer, and the months devoted to food storage now pay off. Winter eventually wanes, and the warmth and life of spring prevails.

An important aspect of seasonality is its effect on the composition of an area's animal population. You will typically see a different group of animals in an area in winter than you will in summer. Many animals, such as ground squirrels, bears, amphibians and reptiles, are dormant in winter. Conversely, ungulates may be more visible in winter because of the lack of foliage and their tendency to enter meadows to find edible vegetation.

TOP WILDLIFE-WATCHING SITES

Although Ontario has only 6 national parks, it boasts 280 provincial parks that protect 7.1 million hectares of habitat—almost 9% of the province. Understandably, providing details on each of these parks is well beyond the scope of this book. A few of Ontario's largest parks are described below. The province's other parks are also worth visiting, including the larger provincial parks of Lake Superior, Lady Evelyn-Smoothwater, Kesagami, Opasquia, Wabakimi and Quetico. These parks have varying degrees of accessibility, but for hardy adventurers, their exploration is a thrilling and rewarding pursuit.

Pukaskwa National Park

The Pukaskwa wilderness of Lake Superior's north shore—part of the ancient Canadian Shield landscape—is a region of forested hills, rough ridges and rocky-shored lakes. The majority of the park is forested, and the dominant trees include spruce, fir, cedar, birch and aspen. Human activity within the park is a concern, because protecting this unique part of Ontario's natural heritage is essential. In this wilderness is a small, isolated population of caribou, as well as good numbers of grey wolves, black bears, moose, mink, Canada lynx and white-tailed deer. Several important research projects have taken place here, studying the interactions between wolves, moose and caribou. Other animals in the park include waterfowl, bald eagles, belted kingfishers, common gartersnakes and painted turtles.

Bruce Peninsula National Park

The dolomite limestone cliffs along the shoreline of the Bruce Peninsula are a part of the spectacular scenery for which this park is famous. Beyond the cliffs is a landscape of mixed forests and wetlands, prime habitat for many wildlife species. The diversity of habitats in this small national park allows for a great variety of plant and animal life. Surprisingly, the Bruce Peninsula is home to 43 species of orchids. The carnivorous pitcher-plant may be found at Dorcas Beach Bay. Hiking, camping, fishing, diving and skiing opportunities abound, and exploring the park provides excellent opportunities for encounters with the local wildlife. Black bears, moose and grey wolves are some of the larger mammals that live within the park boundaries. The Bruce Peninsula is also home to a good number of fishers, and visitors to the park are sometimes rewarded with sightings of these elusive mammals. Scuba divers can visit Canada's first national marine park at the tip of the peninsula to see salmon, chub, bass and crayfish.

Algonquin Provincial Park

The famous Algonquin Park owes much of its scenic beauty to the unique transition environment within its boundaries. Southern areas of the park are mainly deciduous forest, while northern areas mark the beginning of the coniferous boreal forest. The resulting mosaic created by the integration of these 2 zones is a dramatic and diverse biological landscape. The rough topography also influences this mosaic, and throughout the park, you will encounter diverse regions such as maple forest hills, low spruce bogs, lakes, ponds, streams and rocky ridges. Algonquin's excellent accessibility and enormous biological diversity make it one of the finest wildlife-viewing parks in the province. At least 45 mammal species have been recorded here, and Algonquin is the best place in the province to see moose or to listen to the howl of wolves at night. Besides the substantial number of mammal species, the park is home to 272 species of birds, 54 fish species and 31 species of reptiles and amphibians.

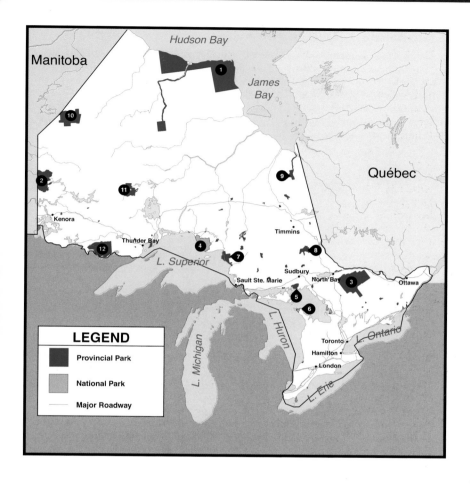

WILDLIFE-WATCHING SITES IN ONTARIO

1. Polar Bear Provincial Park
2. Woodland Caribou Provincial Park
3. Algonquin Provincial Park
4. Pukaskwa National Park
5. Killarney Provincial Park
6. Bruce Peninsula National Park
7. Lake Superior Provincial Park
8. Lady Evelyn-Smoothwater Provincial Park
9. Kesagami Provincial Park
10. Opasquia Provincial Park
11. Wabakimi Provincial Park
12. Quetico Provincial Park

Killarney Provincial Park

The rocky and imposing landscape of Killarney Provincial Park has long been a source of inspiration for artists, including some that became members of the Group of Seven. The patchwork of rocky terrain and coniferous forests gives the classic impression of dramatic wilderness, but this park is easily accessible and is located just southwest of Sudbury. Canoeing and backcountry hiking are the most common activities in the park. Red foxes, northern river otters, moose, white-tailed deer, bobcats, American martens and beavers all inhabit the park, as well as 100 species of migratory or resident birds, 20 species of reptiles and amphibians and many fish species.

Woodland Caribou Provincial Park

As its name suggests, Woodland Caribou Provincial Park supports a large number of caribou. This park is situated along the Manitoba-Ontario border, and access is restricted to air, water or rough forest roads. Canoeing is a major attraction in this park, and the connected lakes and rivers offer more than 1600 km of water routes. The animals found here are those common to the boreal forest. As well, there are a few species present that are typical of more southwestern habitats. Besides caribou, mammals include moose, black bears, northern river otters, wolverines, Canada lynx, red foxes, grey wolves and one of the only well-documented colonies of Franklin's ground squirrels in Ontario. Fish enthusiasts will find walleye, northern pike, muskellunge, bass and lake trout. Almost 100 species of birds, including osprey, terns, pelicans and owls, inhabit the forests, as well as leopard frogs and snapping and painted turtles.

Polar Bear Provincial Park

This park, the most northerly park in Ontario, is accessible only by aircraft. The effort required to get there, however, is worth the reward, because this park protects over 2 million hectares of low-lying, unspoiled tundra. Peat soils and muskeg are found all over the region, and an obvious treeline occurs in the park. North of the treeline, plant life includes caribou lichen and reindeer and sphagnum moss; south of the treeline, there are stunted willows, spruce and tamaracks. Heath carpets the tundra, adding colour in summer and turning red in autumn. Large numbers of caribou live here, and walruses, beluga whales and seals may be sighted in coastal areas and estuaries. Lucky summer visitors may spot snowy owls, peregrine falcons or jaegers. The high density of polar bears in this park in early winter attracts many wildlife enthusiasts, researchers and photographers.

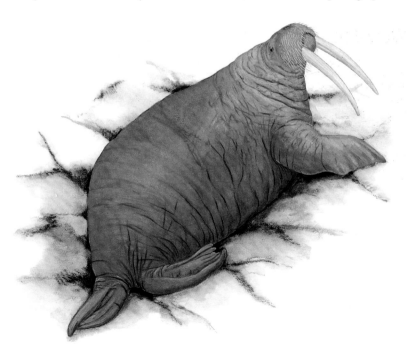

ENJOYING ONTARIO NATURE

Each year, many Ontario residents and tourists enjoy the scenic vistas, fresh air and wilderness that the province's natural areas provide. It is easy to imagine the effect that such a large number of admirers could have on plants, animals and the landscape. Practicing minimum-impact techniques such as those listed below will help keep Ontario clean, beautiful and wild for people, plants and animals:

1. Avoid approaching, harassing or feeding wildlife. Wildlife that learns to associate people with food can become aggressive and dangerous once the animals stop foraging for natural foods. Pets that chase or kill wildlife are best left at home. Dogs should always be kept on a leash. Cats are responsible for the deaths of many songbirds and other small animals each year, so are best kept indoors or on a leash.

2. Stay on marked trails and in designated camping sites. These sites have been hardened to bear the impact of repeated human use. There is minimal impact on vegetation and fewer animal conflicts when people stay on the trails.

3. Bring your eyes to the flower, not the flower to your eyes. Picking flowers and removing them can damage or kill the plant and prevent others from enjoying its beauty. Similar respect should be shown toward fossils, artifacts, antlers and other sources of natural history.

4. Leave wild animals in their natural habitat. Removing wildlife from wild places almost always results in more harm than good.

5. Keep your food secure from animals, keep your cooking materials clean and dispose of your garbage in designated animal-proof containers. Resist littering! Backcountry campers should pack out all of their garbage rather than burying it or leaving it in the backcountry.

6. Respect the rights of landowners and other wildlife viewers. Ask permission to access private lands and respect the rules of public lands.

ANIMALS

Animals are mammals, birds, reptiles, amphibians, fish and invertebrates, all of which belong to the Kingdom Animalia. They obtain energy by ingesting food that they hunt or gather. Mammals and birds are endothermic, meaning that body temperature is internally regulated and will stay nearly constant despite the surrounding environmental temperature unless that temperature is extreme and persistent. Reptiles, amphibians, fish and invertebrates are ectothermic, meaning that they do not have the ability to generate their own internal body temperature and tend to be the same temperature as their surroundings. Animals reproduce sexually, and they have a limited growth that is reached at sexual maturity. They also have diverse and complicated behaviours displayed in courtship, defence, parenting, playing, fighting, eating, hunting, in their social hierarchy, and in how they deal with environmental stresses such as weather, change of season or availability of food and water.

MAMMALS

Mammals are the group to which human beings belong. The general characteristics of a mammal include being endothermic, bearing live young (with the exception of echidnas and the platypus), nursing their young and having hair or fur on their bodies. In general, all mammals larger than rodents are sexually dimorphic, meaning that the male and the female are different in appearance by size or other diagnostics such as antlers. Males are usually larger than females. Different groups of mammals are either herbivores, carnivores, omnivores or insectivores. People often associate large mammals with wilderness, making these animals prominent symbols in native legends and stirring emotional connections with people in modern times.

Marine Mammals
pp. 42–43

Hoofed Mammals
pp. 44–45

Cats
pp. 46–47

Skunks & Weasels
pp. 47–51

Raccoon
p. 51

Bears
p. 52

Dogs
pp. 53–55

Porcupine
p. 55

Mice, Rats & Kin
pp. 56–59

Beaver
p. 59

Squirrels & Kin
pp. 60–62

Hares & Rabbits
pp. 62–63

Bats
pp. 64–66

Moles & Shrews
pp. 67–68

Opossum
p. 69

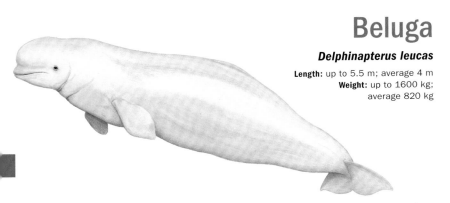

Beluga

Delphinapterus leucas

Length: up to 5.5 m; average 4 m
Weight: up to 1600 kg;
average 820 kg

Lolling on the surface of icy arctic waters, belugas look more like whitecaps than whales. These social animals usually appear in groups, whistling, warbling and squealing to each other as they navigate between chunks of floating ice. Well adapted to frigid waters, belugas are insulated by a thick layer of blubber. Their lack of a dorsal fin also helps them avoid being battered by ice. These graceful white whales have a circumpolar distribution, including several populations in Hudson Bay and a small St. Lawrence River population that occurs as far inland as Québec City. **Where found:** Hudson Bay.

Walrus

Odobenus rosmarus

Length: male up to 3.7 m; female up to 2.9 m
Weight: male up to 1000 kg; female up to 800 kg

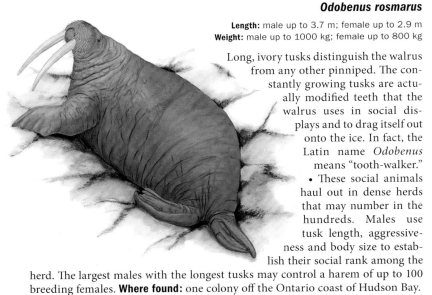

Long, ivory tusks distinguish the walrus from any other pinniped. The constantly growing tusks are actually modified teeth that the walrus uses in social displays and to drag itself out onto the ice. In fact, the Latin name *Odobenus* means "tooth-walker."
• These social animals haul out in dense herds that may number in the hundreds. Males use tusk length, aggressiveness and body size to establish their social rank among the herd. The largest males with the longest tusks may control a harem of up to 100 breeding females. **Where found:** one colony off the Ontario coast of Hudson Bay.

Ringed Seal

Pusa hispida

Length: 1.2–1.7 m
Weight: 50–110 kg

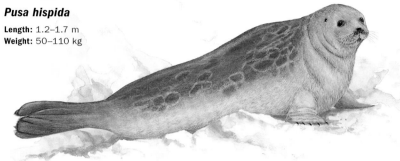

Ringed seals, the smallest and most common seals found in the Arctic, are closely associated with sea ice. • For protection against predators and freezing temperatures during birthing, females hollow out a snow den under ice ridges. The fluffy, white pups are born in spring but turn a silvery grey once they are weaned, at about 8 weeks. At this time, females and pups abandon the den, and large groups bask on the sea ice and moult. Otherwise, ringed seals are largely solitary. • Seals are important to the traditional Inuit culture and diet. Their many predators include polar bears, arctic foxes and walruses. **Where found:** on or near ice; Hudson and James bays.

Bearded Seal

Erignathus barbatus

Length: 2.1–3 m
Weight: 200–350 kg

Bearded seals are named for the long, thick whiskers that they use to search the ocean bottom for food. These benthic feeders prefer shallow water 150–200 m deep, and solitary individuals may show up anywhere along the Ontario coast during ice-free months. They prefer moving ice floes and are seldom seen on land. • During breeding season, males gather on communal display grounds and serenade females. Their trilling calls can last 30 seconds and carry underwater for up to 25 km. • Unlike other seals, females give birth to twins and breed once every 2 years. **Where found:** shallow waters along Hudson and James bays.

North American Elk

Cervus elaphus

Length: 1.8–2.7 m
Shoulder height: 1.7–2.1 m
Weight: 180–500 kg

The impressive bugle of the male North American elk once resounded throughout much of the continent, but the advance of civilization pushed these social animals west. Our native eastern elk (ssp. *canadensis*) had disappeared from Ontario by 1850, and the small elk populations found here today originate from reintroduced western stock. • During the autumn mating season, rival males use their majestic antlers to win and protect a harem of females. After the rut, bull elk can put on as much as half a kilogram per day if conditions are right. The extra weight helps them survive winter. **Where found:** prefers grasslands or open forests; reintroduced near Sudbury, Lake Huron/North Shore, Haliburton Highlands, Frontenac Axis, Ottawa Valley, Lake of the Woods. **Also known as:** wapiti.

White-tailed Deer

Odocoileus virginianus

Length: 1.4–2.1 m
Shoulder height: 70–115 cm
Weight: 30–115 kg

A wagging white tail disappearing into the forest is a common view of this abundant and adaptable deer. • When a mother deer is feeding, it will leave its scentless, spotted fawn behind among tall grasses or shrubs to hide it from potential predators. • A dense network of blood vessels coated by hair, called velvet, covers the developing antlers of males in spring and summer. **Where found:** clearings, young forests, valleys, meadows, farmlands; throughout the southern ⅓ of Ontario. **Also known as:** flag-tailed deer.

Moose

Alces alces

Length: 2.5–3 m
Shoulder height: 1.7–2.1 m
Weight: 230–540 kg

The moose is the largest member of the deer family in the world and is well adapted to northern coniferous forests. Long legs help it wade through bogs or navigate deep patches of snow. It can run as fast as 55 km/h, swim continuously for several hours, dive to depths of 6 m and remain submerged for up to a minute. • A small cluster of aspen trees with the tops snapped off is a sign that a moose stopped by for lunch. In fact, its common name stems from the Algonquin word *moz* or "twig-eater." **Where found:** coniferous forests, young poplar stands, willows; throughout Ontario, except the extreme south.

Caribou

Rangifer tarandus

Length: 1.4–2.3 m
Shoulder height: 0.9–1.7 m
Weight: 90–110 kg

Caribou are amazing animals that migrate hundreds of kilometres over harsh terrain. They draw the energy for their incredible journey from a diet of mainly lichens, grass and moss. Each year, these nomadic animals follow the available food supply, moving between protected winter habitat in the northern coniferous forests and summer calving grounds in the open tundra. Their name originates from the Mi'kmaq word *halibu*, meaning "pawer" or "scratcher," because they feed by digging through the snow with their broad hooves to expose lichens. **Where found:** mature coniferous forests and tundra of northern Ontario.

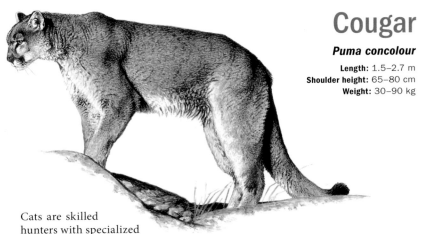

Cougar

Puma concolour

Length: 1.5–2.7 m
Shoulder height: 65–80 cm
Weight: 30–90 kg

Cats are skilled hunters with specialized teeth and claws for capturing prey. A cougar can sink its sharp canines into the neck of a large deer or moose and kill it in one lethal bite. This animal hunts between dusk and dawn, travelling an average of 10 km per night. Historically, the cougar was found throughout the southern Ontario, but as the area was settled, cougars and their prey were pushed out. There are still unconfirmed cougar sightings each year in northern Ontario, but reports from the south are usually attributed to misidentification or escaped pets. **Where found:** remote, forested, rocky areas of northern Ontario. **Also known as:** puma.

Canada Lynx

Lynx canadensis

Length: 80–100 cm
Shoulder height: 45–60 cm
Weight: 7–18 kg

The elusive Canada lynx slinks through remote forests avoiding human settlements, but occasionally appears near rural cottages or farms. Behaving much like a house cat, the lynx will hide in the tall grass to stalk prey or curl up on a comfortable branch for an afternoon siesta. • Lynx populations fluctuate every 7–10 years with snowshoe hare numbers. When hares are plentiful, lynx kittens are more likely to survive and reproduce; when there are fewer hares, more kittens starve and the lynx population declines. **Where found:** coniferous forests north of the French and Mattawa rivers.

Bobcat

Lynx rufus

Length: 75–125 cm
Shoulder height: 45–55 cm
Weight: 7–13 kg

The bobcat has the widest distribution of any native cat in North America and ranges from southern Canada to central Mexico. All bobcats have dark streaks or spots, but their coat varies from yellowish to rusty brown or grey, depending on habitat and season. • These nocturnal hunters use a variety of habitats including deserts, wetlands and mountainous terrain. Bobcats have small feet and are not well adapted to the deep snow of northern Ontario, where the Canada lynx replaces them. Lynx have longer ear tufts and a longer, black-tipped tail. **Where found:** boreal forest from Lake of the Woods and Lake Nipigon south to Algonquin Park.

Striped Skunk

Mephitis mephitis

Length: 53–76 cm
Weight: 1.9–4.2 kg

Equipped with a noxious spray that can be aimed up to 6 m, the striped skunk gives both humans and animals alike an overpowering reason to avoid it. But come spring, when the mother skunk emerges with her fluffy, 2-toned babies trotting behind her, you may find yourself enjoying her company—from a distance. Skunk families typically den in hollow logs or rock piles in summer then switch to old woodchuck or badger burrows for winter. **Where found:** moist urban and rural habitats including hardwood groves and agricultural areas; south from Lake of the Woods, Lake Nipigon and the south end of James Bay, also along the coastlines of Hudson and James bays.

American Marten

Martes americana

Length: 56–66 cm
Weight: 0.5–1.2 kg

Ontario's mature boreal and mixedwood forests are both hunting ground and playground for the agile American marten. This swift, elusive predator may be found stalking mice on the forest floor or scurrying among tree branches to raid a bird's nest. The marten hunts both at night and during the day, feeding mainly on small rodents. It also eats fish, snakes, small birds or eggs, carrion and sometimes berries. • Prized for its soft, luxurious fur, and closely related to the Eurasian sable (*M. zibellina),* trapping combined with habitat loss has contributed to the American marten's decline. **Where found:** mature coniferous forests; throughout Ontario, except the extreme south.

Fisher

Martes pennanti

Length: 79–107 cm
Weight: 2–5.5 kg

Although the fisher is a good swimmer, fish do not make up a large part of its diet. This opportunistic hunter will eat squirrels, hares and birds, and it is one of the few animals that can successfully kill a porcupine by attacking the unprotected head. • The fast, formidable fisher has specially adapted ankle bones that allow it to rotate its feet and climb down trees headfirst. • Chances of seeing this reclusive animal are slim. It prefers tracts of intact wilderness and will disappear once humans invade and development begins. **Where found:** dense coniferous and mixedwood forests; throughout Ontario, except in the extreme south.

Short-tailed Weasel

Mustela erminea

Length: 25–33 cm
Weight: 45–105 g

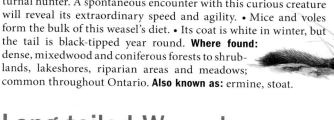

A common inhabitant of coniferous or mixedwood forests and streamside woodlands, the short-tailed weasel is a voracious nocturnal hunter. A spontaneous encounter with this curious creature will reveal its extraordinary speed and agility. • Mice and voles form the bulk of this weasel's diet. • Its coat is white in winter, but the tail is black-tipped year round. **Where found:** dense, mixedwood and coniferous forests to shrublands, lakeshores, riparian areas and meadows; common throughout Ontario. **Also known as:** ermine, stoat.

Long-tailed Weasel

Mustela frenata

Length: 30–46 cm
Weight: 85–400 g

This weasel has adapted to a variety of wild and rural habitats. It feeds on small rodents, birds, insects, reptiles, amphibians and occasionally fruits and berries. It will even prey on species twice its size, including rabbits, muskrats and ground squirrels. • Like other true weasels, it turns white in winter, but the tip of the tail remains black. **Where found:** open, grassy meadows, brushland, woodlots, forest edges and fencerows; throughout the southern ⅓ of Ontario.

Mink

Mustela vison

Length: 47–70 cm
Weight: 0.6–1.4 kg

Graceful, fluid movements set the mink apart from other weasels as it winds like a ribbon along shorelines. Rarely found far from water, the mink's webbed feet make it an excellent swimmer and diver, and it often finds its food underwater. Its thick, dark brown to blackish, oily fur insulates the body from extremely cold waters. • Mink travel along established hunting routes, sometimes resting in a muskrat lodge after eating the original inhabitant. **Where found:** shorelines of lakes, marshes and streams; common throughout Ontario.

Wolverine

Gulo gulo

Length: 70–110 cm
Weight: 7–16 kg

Appearing as a flash of gold between the willows, the wolverine winds between tussocks in search of lemmings or bird nests. This muscular animal is capable of taking down a caribou or moose but usually scavenges carrion left behind by larger predators. With its powerful jaws, the wolverine can crunch through bone to access the nourishing marrow, leaving little trace of a carcass on the bloodstained snow. It also eats small animals, fish and berries. Chances of seeing this elusive animal are slim, even in the most remote areas. **Where found:** remote boreal forest and tundra of northwestern Ontario.

Badger

Taxidea taxus

Length: 64–89 cm
Weight: 5–11 kg

Equipped with huge claws and strong forelimbs, the badger can dig a hole almost in the blink of an eye. Its powerful jaws, long teeth and aggressive defence tactics make it a formidable fighter against most predators. The badger has short legs and a squat, shaggy body. • Badgers have been known to hunt cooperatively with coyotes. • Badger holes are essential in providing den sites, shelters and hibernacula for many creatures, from coyotes to black-widow spiders. **Where found:** low-elevation fields, meadows, grasslands, fence lines and ditches; only 2 populations remain in Ontario, one along the north shore of Lake Erie and another in the Rainy River area.

Northern River Otter

Lontra canadensis

Length: 90–140 cm
Weight: 5–11 kg

If you have ever met a frisky family of otters, you will never forget their playful aquatic antics and games. Their fully webbed feet, long, streamlined bodies and muscular tails make them swift swimmers with incredible fishing ability. • River otters are highly social animals, usually travelling in small groups. Listen for their grunting vocalizations and look for their "slides" on the shores of water bodies. **Where found:** near lakes, ponds and streams; throughout Ontario except in the extreme south.

Raccoon

Procyon lotor

Length: 65–100 cm
Weight: 5–14 kg

The black mask and ringed tail of the raccoon is a familiar sight in many parts of Ontario, including urban and suburban settings. • By watching their mothers, young raccoons learn to handle a wide variety of food items, ranging from shellfish, snakes and small mammals to bird eggs, berries and watermelon. These crafty critters also use their dexterous little paws to pry off well-sealed garbage can lids or undo tent zippers. • Raccoons are known for wetting their food before eating, a behaviour that allows them to feel for and discard inedible matter. **Where found:** wooded areas near water; throughout the southern ½ of Ontario.

Black Bear

Ursus americanus

Length: 1.4–1.8 m
Height: 90–110 cm
Weight: 40–270 kg

Black bears owe their success to a varied diet and the ability to thrive in many environments, from the arctic treeline south to Mexico. • This bear browses mainly on twigs or berries in summer and nuts or roots in autumn, and plants make up ¾ of its diet. These opportunistic and solitary hunters will also consume small animals, insects, fish, carrion and human garbage. • Black bears are excellent climbers whose molar teeth are remarkably similar to those of humans. **Where found:** forests and open, marshy woodlands; throughout Ontario except in the extreme south.

Polar Bear

Ursus maritimus

Length: 2–3.4 m
Height: 1.2–1.6 m
Weight: *Male:* 300–800 kg;
Female: 150–300 kg

Equipped with layers of fat, hollow white guard hairs and absorbent black skin, polar bears are well adapted to icy waters and subzero temperatures. • Cubs are born in midwinter and spend their first 3 months in a snow den, suckling on their mother's warm milk. They emerge in early May and spend their first 28 months with their mother, learning how to survive and hunt seals on the arctic ice packs. Unfortunately, recent climate change models predict drastic changes in the distribution and thickness of the sea ice that polar bears and seals depend on for hunting, denning and resting. **Where found:** on the shores of Hudson and James bays and up to 100 km inland.

Coyote

Canis latrans

Length: 1–1.3 m
Height: 58–66 cm
Weight: 10–22 kg

Occasionally forming loose packs and joining in spirited yipping choruses, coyotes are intelligent and versatile hunter-scavengers. These opportunistic omnivores have greatly expanded their range because of declining grey wolf numbers and favourable habitat changes brought on by forestry and agriculture. Coyotes are found in open woodlands and cultivated lands and near suburban or urban areas, whereas wolves prefer remote, heavily forested regions. • The coyote has a smaller, thinner muzzle than the wolf, and its tail drags behind its legs when it runs. **Where found:** open woodlands, agricultural lands and near urban areas; throughout central and southern Ontario. **Also known as:** brush wolf.

Grey Wolf

Canis lupus

Length: 1.5–2 m
Height: 66–97 cm
Weight: 25–80 kg

The hauntingly beautiful howl of the grey wolf is a unique wilderness sound—and one that is relatively accessible in Algonquin Provincial Park, where "Public Wolf Howls" are part of the summer interpretive program. • Wolf packs cooperate within a strong social structure that is dominated by an alpha pair (top male and female). • Ontario is home to 2 forms of the grey wolf: the larger, variably coloured (white, grey or black) northern wolf (*C. l. occidentalis*) and the smaller, brownish grey southern wolf, also known as the Algonquin wolf or eastern wolf (*C. l. lycaon*). **Where found:** forests and streamside woodlands; throughout Ontario, except in the extreme south. **Also known as:** timber wolf.

Arctic Fox

Alopex lagopus

Length: 75–91 cm
Height: 25–30 cm
Weight: 1.8–4.1 kg

White in the winter and bluish grey in the summer, the arctic fox is the only member of the dog family that changes fur colour with the seasons. Uniquely adapted to the Arctic, this small fox has a dense, insulating coat, furry feet and acute hearing for tracking small animals under the snow. • The arctic fox feeds on polar bear or grey wolf kills, rodents, bird eggs and occasionally seal pups. During the plentiful summer months, this resourceful fox stores food for the winter by digging a hole into the permafrost layer. **Where found:** tundra adjacent to Hudson Bay.

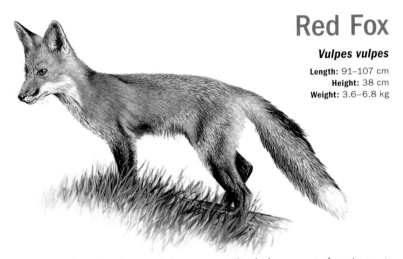

Red Fox

Vulpes vulpes

Length: 91–107 cm
Height: 38 cm
Weight: 3.6–6.8 kg

Red foxes are talented and entertaining mousers that hide or creep along in a cat-like crouch before pouncing on their prey. These playful, adaptive animals have 3 colour morphs: red morph (reddish yellow); black morph (black, often with white-tipped hairs that give a silvery appearance); and cross morph (brown to reddish yellow with a blackish cross down the back and shoulders). All colour morphs have black feet, legs and ear tips, pale underparts and a thick, white-tipped tail. **Where found:** open habitats with brushy shelter, riparian areas and edge habitats; common throughout Ontario.

Grey Fox

Urocyon cinereoargenteus

Length: 76–110 cm
Height: 36–38 cm
Weight: 3.4–5.9 kg

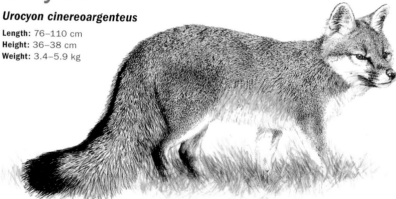

Preferring rocky, shrub-covered terrain and avoiding populated areas, the mainly nocturnal grey fox is seldom seen by humans. Most remarkable is its ability to climb trees to escape danger, pursue birds or find egg-filled nests. The grey fox may even use a high tree cavity for denning. Like other foxes, it is omnivorous.
• The grey fox's fur is shorter and denser than that of the red fox. **Where found:** open forests, shrublands and rocky areas; rare species along the St. Lawrence River west to Georgian Bay; also in the Rainy River area.

Porcupine

Erethizon dorsatum

Length: 66–104 cm
Weight: 3.5–18 kg

Contrary to popular myth, porcupines cannot throw their 30,000 or so quills, but they do rely on a lightning-fast flick of the tail to deliver the quills into persistent attackers.
• Porcupines are excellent tree climbers that feed on forbs, shrubs and the sugary cambium layer of trees. Their insatiable craving for salt occasionally drives them to gnaw on rubber tires, wooden axe handles, toilet seats and even hiking boots! **Where found:** coniferous and mixed deciduous-coniferous forests up to the subalpine; throughout the southern ½ of Ontario.

Meadow Jumping Mouse

Zapus hudsonius

Length: 19–22 cm
Weight: 15–25 g

True to its name, the meadow jumping mouse has large hind feet and a long tail that allow it to hop. It eats in an upright position, grasping food with its petite forelimbs. It is brown in colour, with a dark dorsal stripe, yellowish sides and a white belly. • Meadow jumping mice hibernate for 7–9 months of the year in underground burrows. During their deep sleep, their metabolism slows to a minimum, and they survive solely on the body's fat stores. **Where found:** prefers fields; also forest edges, marshes and streambanks; throughout Ontario.

Woodland Jumping Mouse

Napaeozapus insignis

Length: 20–26 cm
Weight: 17–26 g

The remarkable woodland jumping mouse is capable of making leaps up to 1.8 m in length, an astonishing 18 times the length of its own body. That's roughly equivalent to a human jumping 30 m! Baby jumping mice begin standing on their shaky hind legs about 12 days after birth, and after a month, they are able to leap at least 6 times the length of their bodies. • This tricoloured mouse has a dark brown back, orange sides and white underparts. **Where found:** moist forested regions; from Kenora to Moosonee and south.

Norway Rat

Rattus norvegicus

Length: 30–46 cm
Weight: 200–480 g

Native to Europe and Asia, the Norway rat came to North America as a stowaway on early ships. It mainly associates with human settlements, feeding on cereal grains, fruits, vegetation and garbage. • Norway rats can carry parasites and diseases that are transferable to wildlife, humans, and pets, but captive-bred rats have given psychologists many insights into human learning and behavior. Wild Norway rats have brown to reddish brown, often grizzled pelage with grey tones and grey undersides. **Where found:** urban areas, farmyards and garbage dumps; from Kenora, Thunder Bay and Ottawa south. **Also known as:** brown rat, common rat, sewer rat, water rat.

House Mouse

Mus musculus

Length: 14–19 cm
Weight: 14–25 g

This familiar mouse can be found in populated areas throughout most of North America. Like the Norway rat, it arrived as a stowaway on ships from Europe, quickly spreading across the continent alongside European settlers. • Though the nocturnal house mouse is found in buildings, white-footed and deer mice are more commonly found indoors in Ontario. • The small house mouse has a brownish to blackish grey back and grey undersides. **Where found:** usually associated with human settlements, including urban houses, garages, farmyards, garbage dumps and granaries; throughout the southern ½ of Ontario.

Deer Mouse

Peromyscus maniculatus

Length: 12–18 cm
Weight: 18–35 g

The abundant deer mouse is a seed-eater, but it will eat insects, spiders, caterpillars, fungi, flowers, berries and even some bird eggs. • Unlike most mammals, the male deer mouse often helps the female raise the young. • Deer mice are great climbers. They are also sources of food for many other animals, and less than 5% of wild deer mice live for a complete year. • Deer mice have a distinctly bicoloured tail, a greyish, reddish or tawny brown coat with white undersides and feet. **Where found:** most dry habitats; throughout Ontario except the junction of Hudson and James bays.

White-footed Mouse

Peromyscus leucopus

Length: 15–20 cm
Weight: 15–25 g

These little critters are strong swimmers, and they often brave the water to colonize islands. They have no qualms about raiding your pantry for food and primarily eat nuts, berries, seeds, vegetation and insects. • The white-footed mouse and its close relative the deer mouse are nearly impossible to tell apart. The white-footed mouse is pale to dark reddish brown above, white below and has protruding ears and a bicoloured tail. **Where found:** various habitats, including woodlands, riparian areas, shrubby areas and some farmlands; south of North Bay.

Southern Red-backed Vole

Clethrionomys gapperi

Length: 12–17 cm
Weight: 12–43 g

Active by day in spruce-fir forests and bogs, this vole is easily recognized by its reddish brown back on an otherwise greyish body. Like other voles, it does not hibernate during winter; instead, it tunnels through the subnivean layer—along the ground, under the snow—in search of seeds, nuts and leaves. • Voles are extremely prolific, but populations will vary according to predator populations and available food supplies. **Where found:** mixedwood and coniferous forests, bogs and riparian areas; Bruce Peninsula and north of the Trent Canal.

Meadow Vole

Microtus pennsylvanicus

Length: 14–20 cm
Weight: 18–64 g

Primarily active at night, this common vole can occasionally be seen in the daytime along fencelines, in agricultural fields and on urban meadows. • As a response to high predation rates, meadow voles are ready to breed 3–4 weeks after birth. • The pelage is brown to blackish brown with grey undersides. **Where found:** open woodlands, orchards, agricultural fields, fencelines and marshes; throughout Ontario. **Also known as:** field mouse.

Southern Bog Lemming

Synaptomys cooperi

Length: 12–15 cm
Weight: 21–50 g

A fleeting view of a brown ball of fur racing through a grassy meadow or along the forest floor may be your only sight of this busy rodent. Well-used runways and neatly clipped piles of grass along paths also indicate its presence. The southern bog lemming maintains an extensive network of mossy runways year round and feeds mainly on sedges and grasses. Its close relative, the northern bog lemming (*S. borealis*), inhabits wet alpine tundra and sphagnum bogs in northern Ontario. **Where found:** open forests, grassy meadows, shrub or sedge areas in the southern $^1/_2$ of Ontario.

Muskrat

Ondatra zibethicus

Length: 14–61 cm
Weight: 0.8–1.6 kg

Considered to be a giant vole, the muskrat is an important aquatic creature in freshwater environments. The muskrat's construction of open-water canals and floating houses of aquatic vegetation creates habitats for many species of waterfowl and aquatic plants that could not otherwise survive in dense stands of cattails and sedges. Muskrats feed heavily on cattails, but will also eat a variety of other plants and animals. • The pelage is silvery or reddish brown to blackish. The tail is narrow and flattened. **Where found:** lakes, marshes, ponds, rivers, reservoirs, dugouts and canals; throughout Ontario.

Beaver

Castor canadensis

Length: 91–122 cm
Weight: 16–30 kg

The loud slap of a beaver's tail on water warns of intruders. Beavers are skillful and unrelenting in the construction and maintenance of their dams and lodges. Shrubs and fallen trees serve as both food and building materials. Beavers' long, continuously growing front incisors are perfect tools for gnawing down trees. • A beaver can remain underwater for up to 15 minutes. Its broad, flattened tail is an extremely effective propulsion device. **Where found:** lakes, ponds, marshes and slow-flowing rivers and streams at most elevations; throughout Ontario.

Eastern Chipmunk

Tamias striatus

Length: 23–30 cm
Weight: 66–139 g

This cheerful little gatherer spends much of its time on the ground or in low bushes, collecting seeds, nuts, berries or mushrooms for winter. Chipmunks are not true winter hibernators and wake up several times to feed, even coming above ground in mild weather. Simple ground burrows have a main and a hidden entrance, a storage chamber for food and a sleeping den, but more complex burrows have multiple passages and chambers. **Where found:** urban habitats, forest edges and open deciduous woodlands; throughout the southern ⅔ of Ontario.

Least Chipmunk

Tamias minimus

Length: 17–23 cm
Weight: 35–71 g

This cute and curious rodent is the smallest of our chipmunks. Ontario's 2 chipmunk species can be difficult to tell apart, but populations are separated by different habitat preferences. Least chipmunks are highly adaptable and will live just about any place not already occupied by another species of chipmunk. They are identified by the grey nape and belly and 5 brown-edged dorsal stripes with 2 extending onto the head. The tail is pale orange underneath. **Where found:** campgrounds, coniferous forests, pastures, rocky outcroppings; central Ontario south to Algonquin Park.

Woodchuck

Marmota monar

Length: 46–66 cm
Weight: 1.8–5.4 kg

Woodchucks, the eastern form of the marmot, have a thick body and powerful claws for digging burrows that can be as long as 15 m. They graze along forest edges and clearings, using their sharp incisors to rapidly cut plants, bark and berries. • Woodchucks are true hibernators and spend much of the year tucked away underground. Human development and the clearing of forests has increased habitat for woodchucks. They are now quite common in areas where they used to be fairly rare. **Where found:** meadows, pastures, open woodlands; throughout Ontario. **Also known as:** groundhog.

Red Squirrel

Tamiasciurus hudsonicus

Length: 28–34 cm
Weight: 140–250 g

Intruders beware! This fearless and extremely vocal tree
squirrel may chatter, stomp its feet, flick its tail and scold
you with a piercing cry until you flee from its territory. The
large middens of discarded pine cone scales are evidence of its
buried bounty of food. A more patient squirrel will allow you to
watch it feed on pine cones as though they are corn on the cob. • The short pelage
is rusty red to olive brown with a white undertail. **Where found:** coniferous and
mixed forests; throughout Ontario. **Also known as:** pine squirrel, chickaree.

Eastern Grey Squirrel

Sciurus carolinensis

Length: 43–50 cm
Weight: 400–710 g

Once confined to unspoiled hardwood forests and
rich valleys, bushy-tailed eastern grey squirrels now
thrive in eastern cities. • Active throughout the year, grey
squirrels have a good sense of smell and can even locate nuts
buried under snow. The 10–20% of hidden nuts that are
missed grow into trees. • Eastern grey squirrels come in
2 colour forms, silver grey and solid black; albinos are rare. **Where found:** mature
deciduous or mixed forests with nut-bearing trees; Lake of the Woods to Thunder
Bay to Algonquin Park and south. **Also known as:** black squirrel.

Northern Flying Squirrel

Glaucomys sabrinus

Length: 24–36 cm
Weight: 75–180 g

Long flaps of skin stretched between
the fore and hind limbs (called the
"patagium") and a broad, flattened tail
allow the nocturnal northern flying
squirrel to glide swiftly from tree to tree.
Flying squirrels play an important role in
forest ecology because they dig up and eat
truffles, the fruiting bodies of certain ectomycorrhizal fungi that grow underground. Through its stool, the squirrels spread the beneficial fungi, helping both
the fungi and the forest plants. **Where found:** primarily old-growth coniferous and
mixed forests; from treeline south to the Hamilton area.

Southern Flying Squirrel

Glaucomys volans

Length: 20–26 cm
Weight: 45–100 g

Our 2 flying squirrels occupy different habitats. The northern flying squirrel sticks to the mixed and coniferous woodlands of the boreal forest, whereas the southern flying squirrel is closely associated with deciduous Carolinian forest. It eats the nuts and seeds of oak, beech and maple trees, as well as bird eggs and insects.
• Nocturnal flying squirrels are active throughout the year, but in very cold weather they enter a torpid state. As many as 50 squirrels may huddle together for warmth in a tree cavity. **Where found:** deciduous woodlands; throughout Carolinian forest south of Algonquin Park and Ottawa.

European Hare

Lepus europaeus

Length: 60–75 cm
Weight: 3–4 kg

Believe it or not, the story of the egg-laying Easter Bunny originated from this adaptable little hare. According to Germanic myth, Eostre, the goddess of spring, created a hare by transforming a bird. Ever since this unusual conception, all hares have laid eggs during the week of Easter to thank Eostre and to celebrate their ancestry. European hares have been introduced worldwide. The first Canadian introduction was made in Brantford, Ontario, in 1912. **Where found:** meadows, golf courses, university campuses, agricultural lands close to hedgerows; south of Ottawa.

Snowshoe Hare

Lepus americanus

Length: 38–53 cm
Weight: 1–1.5 kg

These primarily nocturnal hares have large, snowshoe-like hind feet that allow them to leap across the snow while predators fall behind, sinking. • Snowshoe hares are camouflaged greyish, reddish or blackish brown in summer, but their coats turn white in winter. This adaptation helps a motionless hare avoid predators. If detected, the hare explodes into a running zigzag pattern in its flight for cover, reaching speeds of up to 50 km/h on hard-packed snow trails. **Where found:** brushy or forested area; throughout Ontario except extreme south. **Also known as:** varying hare.

Eastern Cottontail

Sylvilagus floridanus

Length: 40–45 cm
Weight: 0.8–1.6 kg

The eastern cottontail is the smallest of our lagomorphs and the only rabbit in Ontario (the other 3 species are hares). Rabbits have short hind legs, occupy a variety of habitats and dig burrows, giving birth to naked, helpless young. Hares have large hind legs for running, prefer open habitats, rarely burrow and give birth to furry, independent young. • The eastern cottontail has been introduced throughout North America. It breeds year round, with up to 9 bunnies per litter. Females can breed again within hours of giving birth. **Where found:** variety of habitats near shrubby cover; south of North Bay.

Northern Bat

Myotis septentrionalis

Length: 8.3–10 cm
Forearm length: 3.3–4 cm
Weight: 3.5–8.9 g

With almost 1000 species found worldwide, bats are the most successful mammals next to rodents. Ontario's 8 bats all belong to the evening bat family (Vespertilionidae). Members of this family are most active at dusk and dawn, and all are insectivorous, except for a few fish-eating tropical species. • Northern bats are found in both coniferous and deciduous forests, close to water. **Where found:** roosts in natural tree cavities or under peeling tree bark; hibernates in caves or abandoned mines; throughout the southern ½ of Ontario.

Little Brown Bat

Myotis lucifugus

Length: 7–10 cm
Forearm length: 3.5–4.1 cm
Weight: 5.3–8.9 g

These common bats form large maternal roosting colonies each summer to give birth and raise young. Virtually helpless at birth, the single offspring spends its first few days clinging to the chest of its mother until it is strong enough to remain at the roost site. • A single little brown bat can consume 900 insects per hour. **Where found:** roosts in buildings, barns, caves, rock crevices, hollow trees and under tree bark; hibernates in buildings, caves and old mines; throughout the southern ⅔ of Ontario.

Eastern Small-footed Bat

Myotis leibii

Length: 7.2–8.4 cm
Forearm length: 3.0–3.4 cm
Weight: 3–8 g

Little is known about this small, rare bat. This nocturnal feeder is always found near water, swooping over ponds or streams to capitalize on night-flying insects. It prefers hilly areas and is found in both deciduous and coniferous forests, as well as open agricultural land or meadows. • The genus name *Myotis* means "mouse-eared." **Where found:** always near water; roosts under bridges, rock ledges or building eaves; individuals hibernate in crevices and groups hibernate in caves or abandoned mines; spotty distribution from Algonquin Park south.

Eastern Red Bat

Lasiurus borealis

Length: 8.7–12.6 cm
Forearm length: 3.7–4.2 cm
Weight: 7–15 g

These bats lead solitary, inconspicuous lives. Occasionally you might see one illuminated under a streetlight, feeding on insects attracted to the light. Look for its yellowish orange to red fur; the male's fur is a much brighter red.
• This fast flier has long, slender wings and can reach speeds of up to 65 km/h. **Where found:** roosts on unobstructed branches that allow the bat to drop into flight; migrates south for the winter; throughout the southern ⅔ of Ontario but most common south of Algonquin Park.

Hoary Bat

Lasiurus cinereus

Length: 11–15 cm
Forearm length: 4.5–5.7 cm
Weight: 19–35 g

This beautiful bat is an oddball among its kind—both males and females live solitary lives, with females usually giving birth to 2 young. They roost in trees, not caves or buildings, and wrap their wings around themselves for protection against the elements. Hoary bats often roost in orchards, but they are insectivores and do not damage fruit crops. At night, they can be identified by their large size and slow wingbeats over open terrain. **Where found:** roosts on the branches of coniferous and deciduous trees and occasionally in tree cavities; migrates south for the winter; throughout the southern ½ of Ontario.

Silver-haired Bat

Lasionycteris noctivagans

Length: 9–11 cm
Forearm length: 3.8–4.5 cm
Weight: 7–18 g

The silver-haired bat is similar to the hoary bat in its habit of roosting in trees, but it can be found in small, loose groups. It takes flight about half an hour after sunset to patrol open fields, water surfaces, or treetops for prey. To conserve energy on cold days, it can lower its body temperature and metabolism—a state known as "torpor." • This bat's black flight membrane can span 30 cm. **Where found:** roosts in cavities and crevices of old-growth trees; migrates south for the winter; throughout the southern ½ of Ontario.

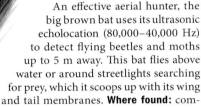

Big Brown Bat

Eptesicus fuscus

Length: 9–14 cm
Forearm length: 4.6–5.4 cm
Weight: 12–28 g

An effective aerial hunter, the big brown bat uses its ultrasonic echolocation (80,000–40,000 Hz) to detect flying beetles and moths up to 5 m away. This bat flies above water or around streetlights searching for prey, which it scoops up with its wing and tail membranes. **Where found:** common in and around artificial structures, occasionally roosting in hollow trees and rock crevices; hibernates in caves, mines and old buildings; from Lake of the Woods and Lake Nipigon to North Bay area and south.

Eastern Pipistrelle

Pipistrellus subflavus

Length: 8–9 cm
Forearm length: 3.1–3.5 cm
Weight: 6 g

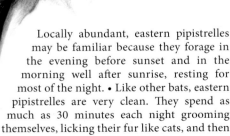

Locally abundant, eastern pipistrelles may be familiar because they forage in the evening before sunset and in the morning well after sunrise, resting for most of the night. • Like other bats, eastern pipistrelles are very clean. They spend as much as 30 minutes each night grooming themselves, licking their fur like cats, and then moistening their hindfeet to reach the remaining areas. **Where found:** always near water; roosts and hibernates in caves, mines, crevices and old buildings.

Hairy-tailed Mole

Parascalops breweri

Length: 14–17 cm
Weight: 40–64 g

Moles spend nearly all their time in
the dark, tunnelling underground with
their large, shovel-like feet and claws. Their
eyes are greatly diminished, as there is not a lot to
see in the dark. Instead, moles use a heightened sense of
touch and hearing to guide them. The hairy-tailed mole prefers
sturdy, sandy loam soils and avoids soils that are too moist or have too much clay.
• It is grey or black above, pale below, and as its name suggests, has a short, hairy
tail. **Where found:** well-drained soils in woodlands, brushy areas or meadows;
from North Bay/Sudbury area south.

Star-nosed Mole

Condylura cristata

Length: 15–21 cm
Weight: 30–75 g

Looking like it collided headfirst with a tiny sea
anemone, the star-nosed mole is a unique exam-
ple of animal diversity. An extremely sensitive
ring of 22 "feelers" covers this mole's snout. Each
fleshy appendage can be collapsed or extended
individually, but moves continuously in all direc-
tions to take in the mole's surroundings. **Where found:**
prefers wet areas such as marshes, low fields or humid woodlands;
throughout the southern ½ of Ontario, but may range farther north.

Masked Shrew

Sorex cinereus

Length: 7–11 cm
Weight: 2–7 g

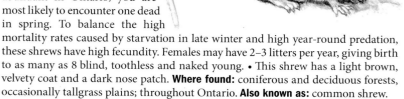

Although the masked shrew is
abundant in Ontario, you are
most likely to encounter one dead
in spring. To balance the high
mortality rates caused by starvation in late winter and high year-round predation,
these shrews have high fecundity. Females may have 2–3 litters per year, giving birth
to as many as 8 blind, toothless and naked young. • This shrew has a light brown,
velvety coat and a dark nose patch. **Where found:** coniferous and deciduous forests,
occasionally tallgrass plains; throughout Ontario. **Also known as:** common shrew.

Common Water Shrew

Sorex palustris

Length: 13–17 cm
Weight: 9–19 g

Large hind feet fitted with stiff, bristly hairs and thick body fur that insulates by trapping air bubbles between the hairs allow the water shrew to hunt aquatic invertebrates in cold ponds and streams. Its larger size and specialized aquatic adaptations also allow it to catch and eat small fish and tadpoles that other shrews cannot. • The coat is dark, velvety brown to black with whitish grey undersides and a distinctive, bicoloured tail. **Where found:** lakes, ponds, marshes and streams with vegetated shorelines; throughout Ontario except in the extreme south. **Also known as:** northern water shrew.

Pygmy Shrew

Sorex hoyi

Length: 11–13 cm
Weight: 2–7 g

Weighing no more than a penny, the pygmy shrew is considered to be the smallest of all North American mammals. The dwarf shrew (*S. nanus*) may weigh less, but it is longer than the pygmy shrew. • Although small, this shrew is voracious: one female on record ate about 3 times her body weight each day for 10 days. The pygmy shrew may also be one of the rarest shrews in North America. **Where found:** throughout Ontario except in the extreme south.

Northern Short-tailed Shrew

Blarina brevicauda

Length: 9.6–14 cm
Weight: 14–29 g

Venomous snakes are familiar to most people, but have you ever heard of a poisonous shrew? The northern short-tailed shrew uses its poisonous saliva to kill and paralyze prey. Rather than injecting venom, short-tailed shrews "chew" poison into their victims, an adaptation that allows them to attack larger rodents and even young rabbits in addition to invertebrates. • These shrews are easily identified by their large size, grey pelage and short tail. **Where found:** variety of habitats including forests, fields and marshes; throughout the southern ½ of Ontario.

Virginia Opossum

Didelphis virginiana

Length: 69–84 cm
Weight: 1.1–1.6 kg

A maternal pouch, opposable "thumbs" and a scaly, prehensile tail characterize the opossum. Few people realize that this animal is Canada's only marsupial, and that the honeybee-sized babies begin life as one of the smallest mammals in North America. • This animal is most famous for feigning death, or "playing possum," when attacked. • Many children's stories illustrate the opossum hanging upside down in trees, actually an unlikely behaviour unless the animal has slipped or is reaching for something. **Where found:** most common in agricultural lands south of Waterloo and Guelph; range may expand northward in mild winters.

BIRDS

A ll birds are feathered, but not all fly. The most diverse class of vertebrates, birds are bipedal, warm-blooded and lay hard-shelled eggs. Some birds migrate south in the colder winter months and return north in spring. For this reason, Ontario has a different diversity of birds in summer than in winter. Many migrating birds fly as far south as Central and South America. Migrants are of concern to biologists and conservationists because pesticide use, decreasing habitat and numerous other problems in both North and South America threaten the survival of many species. Education and increasing appreciation for wildlife may encourage solutions to this problem.

Waterfowl
pp. 72–75

Grouse
p. 76

Diving Birds
p. 77

Herons & Vultures
pp. 78–79

Birds of Prey
pp. 80–81

Cranes
p. 82

Shorebirds
pp. 82–83

Gulls & Terns
pp. 84–85

Pigeons, Doves &
Cuckoos, p. 86

Owls
pp. 87–88

Nighthawks & Swifts
pp. 88–89

Hummingbirds & Kingfishers
p. 89

Woodpeckers
pp. 90–91

Flycatchers
pp. 92–93

Shrikes & Vireos
p. 93

Jays & Crows
pp. 94–95

Larks & Swallows
pp. 95–96

Chickadees & Nuthatches
pp. 96–97

Wrens & Kinglets
pp. 97–98

Thrushes
pp. 98–99

Mimics, Starlings & Waxwings
pp. 99–100

Wood-warblers & Tanagers
pp. 101–02

Sparrows
pp. 103–04

Grosbeaks & Buntings
pp. 104–05

Blackbirds & Allies
pp. 105–06

Finch-like Birds
pp. 107–08

Canada Goose

Branta canadensis

Length: 92–122 cm
Wingspan: up to 1.8 m

At dusk, Canada geese fly in V-formation back to water after a day of foraging. The echo of their honking is a prevalent Ontario sound. • A pair of Canada geese will remain together for life, each year raising, teaching and aggressively defending 2–11 young. • The Canada goose was split into 2 species in 2004. The larger sub-species are known as Canada geese, while the smaller subspecies have been renamed cackling geese. **Where found:** lakeshores, riverbanks, ponds, farmlands and city parks; breeds throughout Ontario, overwinters in the south.

Tundra Swan

Cygnus columbianus

Length: 1.2–1.5 m
Wingspan: 1.8–2.1 m

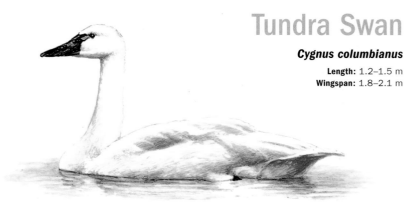

A wave of tundra swans flying overhead is a sight you will never forget. As waters begin to thaw in early March, these noisy swans migrate through Ontario. They gather at staging areas, where they rest and refuel on waste grain and aquatic vegetation. A good time to visit a staging site is in the evening, when hundreds of swans take flight to feed in nearby fields. Tens of thousands of tundra swans migrate over Ontario, but only a handful of pairs nest in northern Ontario. **Where found:** shallow areas of lakes and wetlands; also agricultural fields and flooded pastures; southern and northern Ontario, absent from central Ontario.

Mallard

Anas platyrhynchos

Length: 51–71 cm
Wingspan: 76 cm

The male Mallard, with his shiny green head and chestnut brown breast, is the classic wild duck. Mallards can be seen year round, often in flocks and always near open water. • After breeding, male ducks lose their elaborate plumage, helping them stay camouflaged during their flightless period. In early fall, they moult back into breeding colours. • Most people think of the Mallard's quack as the classic duck call. **Where found:** lakes, wetlands, rivers, city parks, agricultural areas and sewage lagoons; throughout Ontario.

Blue-winged Teal

Anas discors

Length: 36–41 cm
Wingspan: 58 cm

These speedy ducks can be identified by their small size and by the sharp twists and turns they execute in flight. Blue-winged teals and other dabbling ducks feed by tipping up their tails and dunking their heads underwater. • Dabbling ducks have small feet situated near the centre of their bodies. Other ducks, such as scaups, scoters and buffleheads, dive underwater to feed, propelled by large feet set farther back on their bodies. **Where found:** shallow lake edges and wetlands; prefers areas with short but dense emergent vegetation; common breeder throughout Ontario.

Black Scoter

Melanitta nigra

Length: 43–53 cm
Wingspan: 71 cm

Scoters are dark-plumaged sea ducks with brightly coloured, bulbous bills. Three species occur in Ontario. Watch for a line of scoters flying close to the water's surface or small groups feeding over open water. • The male black scoter is the only adult duck in North American with entirely black plumage. Though American coots (*Fulica americana*) are also black-plumaged waterfowl, coots belong to the rail family and are found in freshwater wetlands. **Where found:** common in summer off the north coast of Lake Erie and Lake Ontario.

Bufflehead

Bucephala albeola

Length: 33–38 cm
Wingspan: 53 cm

With its simple, bold plumage, the tiny bufflehead resembles few other waterfowl species. The striking white patch on the rear of the male's head stands out, even at a distance. • Buffleheads often nest in tree cavities, using abandoned wood-pecker nests or natural holes. After hatching, the ducklings remain in the nest chamber for up to 3 days before jumping out and tumbling to the ground. **Where found:** large, open waterbodies; uncommon breeder; common migrant; overwinters along Lake Erie and Lake Ontario shorelines.

Common Goldeneye

Bucephala clangula

Length: 41–51 cm
Wingspan: 66 cm

The common goldeneye spends its entire life in North America, dividing its time between breeding grounds in the boreal forests of Canada and Alaska and its winter territory in marine bays and estuaries along the Atlantic and Pacific coasts. Many also overwinter off the shorelines of the Great Lakes, but numbers depend on food availability and open water. • Common goldeneyes are frequently called "whistlers," because the wind whistles through their wings when they fly. **Where found:** lakes, large ponds and rivers near mature forest; breeds throughout Ontario except in the extreme north.

Common Merganser

Mergus merganser

Length: 56–69 cm
Wingspan: 86 cm

Lumbering like a jumbo jet, the common merganser must run along the surface of the water, beating its heavy wings to gain sufficient lift to take off. Once up and away, this large duck flies arrow-straight and low over the water, making broad, sweeping turns to follow the meandering shorelines of rivers and lakes. These skilled divers are rarely seen on land. **Where found:** large rivers and deep lakes bordered by forest; breeds throughout Ontario; overwinters along the shores of Georgian Bay, Lake Erie and Lake Ontario.

Ruffed Grouse

Bonasa umbellus

Length: 38–48 cm
Wingspan: 56 cm

The male ruffed grouse "drums" to announce his territory, sending a low "booming" echo through the forest. Every spring, and occasionally in fall, the male grouse struts along a fallen log with his tail fanned and his neck feathers ruffed, beating the air periodically with accelerating wing strokes. • Ruffed grouse occur as far north as Alaska. In winter, scales grow out along the sides of their feet, creating temporary "snowshoes." **Where found:** deciduous and mixed forests and riparian woodlands; occurs year round throughout Ontario, except in the northeastern corner.

Spruce Grouse

Length: 33–41 cm
Wingspan: 56 cm

Approachable spruce grouse are more commonly known as "fool hens." They are most conspicuous in late April and early May, when females issue their vehement calls and strutting males magically appear in open areas along walking trails, roads and campgrounds. Look for the spruce grouse's short, pointed tail and the male's black breast to distinguish it from the ruffed grouse. **Where found:** usually in moist, coniferous forests with a dense understorey; common year-round resident north of the North Bay area.

Common Loon

Gavia immer

Length: 71–89 cm
Wingspan: 1.2–1.5 m

The haunting call of the common
loon is synonymous with cottage country. These beautiful diving birds are well
suited to their aquatic lifestyle. Their nearly solid bones decrease their buoyancy
(most birds have hollow bones), and their feet are placed well back on their bodies
to aid in underwater propulsion. Small bass, perch and sunfish are all fair game
for these excellent underwater hunters that will chase fish to depths of up to 55 m.
Where found: large lakes and rivers; breeds throughout Ontario except the
extreme south; overwinters rarely in the Great Lakes.

Pied-billed Grebe

Podilymbus podiceps

Length: 30–38 cm
Wingspan: 41 cm

Relatively solid bones and the
ability to partially deflate its air sac
allow the pied-billed grebe to sink below the surface of the water like a tiny sub-
marine. The inconspicuous grebe can float low in the water or submerge with only
its nostrils and eyes showing above the surface. • Dark plumage, individually
webbed toes and a chicken-like bill distinguish the pied-billed grebe from other
waterfowl. **Where found:** ponds, marshes and backwaters with sparse emergent
vegetation; uncommon breeder and fairly common migrant in the southern ½ and
western regions of Ontario.

Double-crested Cormorant

Phalacrocorax auritus

Length: 66–81 cm
Wingspan: 1.3 m

The double-crested cormorant looks like a bird but smells and swims
like a fish. With a long, rudder-like tail and excellent underwater vision,
this slick-feathered bird has mastered the underwater world. Most
water birds have waterproof feathers, but the structure of the
double-crested cormorant's feathers allow water in. "Wettable"
feathers make this bird less buoyant, which in turn makes it
a better diver. The double-crested cormorant also has sealed
nostrils for diving, and therefore must fly with its bill
open. **Where found:** large lakes; summer resident in the
southern ⅔ of Ontario.

Great Blue Heron

Ardea herodias

Length: 1.3–1.4 m
Wingspan: 1.8 m

This long-legged heron has a stealthy, often motionless hunting strategy. It waits for a fish or frog to approach, spears the prey with its bill, then flips its catch into the air and swallows it whole. Herons usually hunt near water, but they also stalk fields and meadows in search of rodents. • Great blue herons settle in communal treetop nests called rookeries. Nesting herons are sensitive to human disturbance, so observe this bird's behaviour from a distance. **Where found:** forages along edges of rivers, lakes and marshes; also in fields and wet meadows; common breeder throughout the province, except the extreme north; overwinters south of Algonquin Park.

Green Heron

Butorides virescens

Length: 38–56 cm

Wingspan: 66 cm

Sentinel of mangrove or marsh, the ever-vigilant green heron sits hunched on a shaded branch at the water's edge. It often perches just above the water's surface along wooded streams, waiting to stab small fish or other prey with its sturdy, dagger-like bill. • In Asia, green herons have been observed to drop feathers, leaves or other small debris into the water to attract fish, which are then captured and eaten. This makes the green heron one of the few birds known to use tools. **Where found:** marshes, lakes and streams with dense shoreline or emergent vegetation; breeds south of North Bay and in Lake of the Woods area.

Black-crowned Night-Heron

Nycticorax nycticorax

Length: 58–66 cm
Wingspan: 1.1 m

When the long shadows of dusk shroud the wetlands, black-crowned night-herons arrive to hunt in the marshy waters. These herons crouch motionless, using their large, light-sensitive eyes to spot prey lurking in the shallows. *Nycticorax,* meaning "night raven," refers to this bird's distinctive nighttime calls. • The black-crowned night-heron is the most abundant heron in the world, occurring virtually world-wide. Watch for it in summer, between dawn and dusk, as it flies from its nesting colony to feeding areas and back. **Where found:** shallow cattail and bulrush marshes, lakeshores and along slow rivers; breeds south of Algonquin Park.

Turkey Vulture

Cathartes aura

Length: 66–81 cm
Wingspan: 1.7–1.8 m

Turkey vultures are intelligent, playful and social birds. Groups live and sleep together in large trees, or "roosts." Some roost sites are over a century old and have been used by the same family of vultures for several generations. • No other bird uses updrafts and thermals in flight as well as the turkey vulture. Pilots have reported seeing vultures soaring at altitudes of over 6000 m. • A threatened turkey vulture will play dead or throw up. The odour of its vomit repulses attackers, much like the odour of a skunk's spray. **Where found:** usually flies over open country, shorelines or roads; rarely over forests; breeds in southern Ontario.

Osprey

Pandion haliaetus

Length: 56–64 cm
Wingspan: 1.7–1.8 m

The large and powerful osprey occurs on every continent except Antarctica and is almost always found near water. • A hunting osprey will hover over the water before hurling itself downward in a dramatic headfirst dive, then suddenly pull out and thrust its feet forward to grasp prey. This fish-eater has specialized feet for gripping slippery prey—2 toes point forward, 2 point backward and all are covered with sharp spines. • Ospreys build bulky stick nests on high, artificial structures such as communication towers and utility poles, or on buoys over water. **Where found:** lakes and rivers; breeds throughout Ontario.

Bald Eagle

Haliaeetus leucocephalus

Length: 79–109 cm
Wingspan: 1.7–2.4 m

This majestic sea eagle hunts mostly fish and is often found near water. While soaring high in the air, an eagle can spot fish swimming underwater and small rodents scurrying through the grass. Bald eagles also scavenge carrion and steal food from other birds. • Bald eagles do not mature until their fourth or fifth year—only then do they develop the characteristic white head and tail plumage. These birds mate for life and renew pair bonds by adding sticks to their nests, which can be up to 4.5 m in diameter (the largest of any North American bird). **Where found:** large lakes and rivers; breeds throughout Ontario.

Northern Harrier

Circus cyaneus

Length: 41–61 cm
Wingspan: 1.1–1.2 m

With its prominent white rump and distinctive, slightly upturned wings, the northern harrier may be the easiest raptor to identify in flight. Unlike other midsized birds, it often flies close to the ground, relying on sudden surprise attacks to capture prey. • Britain's Royal Air Force was so impressed by the northern harrier's maneuverability that it named the Harrier aircraft after this bird. **Where found:** open country, including fields, wet meadows and cattail marshes; breeds throughout Ontario; rare winter resident in the south.

Broad-winged Hawk

Buteo platypterus

Length: 36–48 cm
Wingspan: 81–99 cm

The best time to see broad-winged hawks in
Ontario is during fall migration, when "kettles" of these buteos
migrate south to wintering grounds in Central and South America. Hundreds or even thousands of these hawks take advantage of
warm, thermal air currents to soar, sometimes gliding for hours without flapping.
• This shy hawk shuns open fields and forest clearings, preferring dense, often wet
forests. Its short, broad wings and highly flexible tail help it to maneuver in the
heavy growth. **Where found:** dense mixed and deciduous forests; southern ⅔ of
Ontario.

Red-tailed Hawk

Buteo jamaicensis

Length: *Male:* 46–58 cm; *Female:* 51–64 cm
Wingspan: 1.2–1.5 m

Red-tails are the most common hawks in Ontario, especially
in winter. In warm weather, these hawks use thermals and
updrafts to soar. The pockets of rising air provide substantial lift,
which can allow migrating hawks to fly for 3 km without flapping their wings. • The Red-tailed hawk's piercing call is often
paired with the image of an eagle in TV commercials and movies. **Where
found:** open country with some trees; also roadsides or woodlots; breeds
throughout Ontario except in the extreme north; overwinters in the south.

American Kestrel

Falco sparverius

Length: 19–20 cm
Wingspan: 51–61 cm

The colourful American kestrel, formerly known
as the "sparrow hawk," is a common and widespread falcon, not shy of human activity and
adaptable to habitat change. This small falcon
has benefited from the grassy rights-of-way created by Ontario's highways, which provide habitat for
grasshoppers and other small prey. Watch for this robin-sized bird along rural
roadways, perched on poles and telephone wires, or over agricultural fields, foraging for insects and small mammals. **Where found:** open fields, riparian woodlands
and croplands; breeds throughout Ontario except in the extreme north; overwinters in the south.

Sandhill Crane

Grus canadensis

Length: 1.1–1.2 m
Wingspan: 1.8–2.1 m

The sandhill crane's deep, rattling call can be heard long before this bird passes overhead. Its coiled trachea alters the pitch of its voice, making it sound louder and carry farther.
• At first glance, large, V-shaped flocks of sandhill cranes look like flocks of Canada geese, but the cranes often soar and circle in the air, and they do not honk like geese.
• Cranes mate for life and reinforce pair bonds each spring with an elaborate courtship dance that looks somewhat like human dancing. **Where found:** *Breeding:* isolated, shrubby marshes, bogs and coastal tundra of northeastern Ontario. *In migration:* agricultural fields and shorelines.

Killdeer

Charadrius vociferus

Length: 23–28 cm
Wingspan: 61 cm

The killdeer is a gifted actor, well known for its "broken wing" distraction display. When an intruder wanders too close to its nest, the killdeer greets the interloper with piteous cries while dragging a wing and stumbling about as if injured. Most predators take the bait and follow, and once the killdeer has lured the predator far away from its nest, it miraculously recovers from the injury and flies off with a loud call. **Where found:** breeds throughout Ontario in open fields, lakeshores, gravel streambeds and abandoned industrial areas.

Spotted Sandpiper

Actitis macularius

Length: 18–20 cm
Wingspan: 38 cm

The female spotted sandpiper, unlike most other female birds, lays her eggs and leaves the male to tend the clutch. She diligently defends her territory and may mate with several different males, an unusual breeding strategy known as "polyandry." Each summer, the female can lay up to 4 clutches and is capable of producing 20 eggs. • Spotted sandpipers bob their tails constantly on shore and fly with rapid, shallow, stiff-winged strokes. **Where found:** shorelines, gravel beaches, swamps and sewage lagoons; common migrant and breeder throughout Ontario.

Greater Yellowlegs

Tringa melanoleuca

Length: 33–38 cm
Wingspan: 71 cm

The greater yellowlegs and lesser yellowlegs (*T. flavipes*) are medium-sized sandpipers with very similar plumages; they share the yellow legs and feet that give them their common name. A solitary yellowlegs is difficult to identify until it flushes and utters its distinctive 3 peeps (the lesser yellowlegs peeps twice). The greater yellowlegs is the larger species. Its bill is slightly longer than the length of its head and may have a grey base. **Where found:** shallow wetlands, shorelines and flooded fields; common migrant and breeder throughout Ontario.

Wilson's Snipe

Gallinago delicata

Length: 27–29 cm
Wingspan: 46 cm

When flushed from cover, snipes perform a series of aerial zigzags to confuse predators. Because of this habit, hunters who were skilled enough to shoot snipes became known as "snipers," a term later adopted by the military. • Courting snipes make an eerie, winnowing sound, like a rapidly hooting owl. The male's specialized outer tail feathers vibrate rapidly in the air as he performs daring, headfirst dives high above a wetland. • The similar American woodcock (*Scolopax minor*) is plumper, has unmarked plumage and breeds in southern Ontario only. **Where found:** breeds in marshes, meadows and wetlands throughout Ontario.

Bonaparte's Gull

Larus philadelphia

Length: 30–36 cm
Wingspan: 84 cm

The small and delicate Bonaparte's gull breeds in northern coniferous forests that border lakes. In Ontario, it is most commonly seen during migration. • Bonaparte's gulls are very buoyant, riding high on the water. In flight, they appear rather tern-like, not ponderous like most other gulls. The white primary wedges on the wings of adults are conspicuous, and nonbreeding and juvenile plumages have a black spot behind each eye. **Where found:** *In migration* and *winter:* near large lakes and rivers. *Breeding:* boreal forests.

Ring-billed Gull

Larus delawarensis

Length: 46–51 cm
Wingspan: 1.2 m

Few people can claim that they have never seen this common and widespread gull. Highly tolerant of humans, ring-billed gulls will eat almost anything and will swarm parks, beaches, golf courses and fast-food restaurant parking lots looking for food handouts. They are a three-year gull, first acquiring adult plumage in their third calendar year of life, after going through a series of subadult moults. **Where found:** *Breeding:* bare, rocky and shrubby islands and sewage ponds. *In migration* and *winter:* lakes, rivers, land-fills, parking lots, fields and parks.

Herring Gull

Larus argentatus

Length: 58–66 cm
Wingspan: 1.2 m

Unbelievably, the egg and feather trade extirpated these gulls from southern Ontario in the 1800s. Populations recovered mainly by adapting to feed on human refuse. Today, herring gulls can be locally abundant at landfills, beaches or other areas with great amounts of prey or garbage. On their breeding grounds, herring gulls can be great predators of nestling terns. • Like many gulls, herring gulls have a small red spot on their lower mandible that serves as a target for nestlings. When a chick pecks at the red spot, the parent recognizes the cue and regurgitates a meal. **Where found:** large lakes, wetlands, rivers, landfills and urban areas; breeds throughout Ontario.

Black Tern

Chlidonias niger

Length: 23–25 cm
Wingspan: 61 cm

Black terns rule the skies above cattail marshes. These acrobatic birds wheel about in feeding flights, picking minnows from the water's surface and catching insects in midair. Wetland habitat loss and degradation have caused black tern populations to decline. These birds are sensitive nesters and will not return to a nesting area if the water level or plant density changes. Wetland conservation efforts may eventually help them recover to their former prosperity. **Where found:** shallow marshes, wet meadows, sewage ponds with emergent vegetation; breeds in the southern ⅓ of Ontario.

Common Tern

Sterna hirundo

Length: 33–41 cm
Wingspan: 76 cm

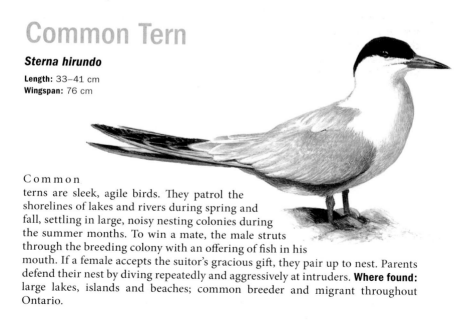

Common terns are sleek, agile birds. They patrol the shorelines of lakes and rivers during spring and fall, settling in large, noisy nesting colonies during the summer months. To win a mate, the male struts through the breeding colony with an offering of fish in his mouth. If a female accepts the suitor's gracious gift, they pair up to nest. Parents defend their nest by diving repeatedly and aggressively at intruders. **Where found:** large lakes, islands and beaches; common breeder and migrant throughout Ontario.

Rock Pigeon

Columba livia

Length: 31–33 cm
Wingspan: 71 cm (male is usually larger)

The rock pigeon is the common city pigeon known to all. This Old World pigeon has been domesticated for about 6500 years. Wild rock pigeons breed on cliffs, but their feral, urban counterparts nest on building ledges or under bridges. • All pigeons and doves feed "pigeon milk" to their young. It is not true milk, of course, but a nutritious liquid produced in the bird's crop. No other bird feeds its young in such a manner. **Where found:** urban areas, railway yards and agricultural areas; very common year-round resident in the southern ⅓ of Ontario.

Mourning Dove

Zenaida macroura

Length: 28–33 cm
Wingspan: 46 cm

The mourning dove is one of the most abundant and wide-spread native birds in North America. There are usually only 2 eggs in the average clutch, but each pair of doves raises multiple broods each breeding season, which is nearly year round in warmer climates. • When the mourning dove bursts into flight, its wings often create a whistling sound. • Its softly repeated *coo* sounds much like a hooting owl. **Where found:** open and riparian woodlands, agricultural and suburban areas, open parks; breeds in southern ½ of Ontario; year round in the extreme south.

Yellow-billed Cuckoo

Coccyzus americanus

Length: 28–33 cm
Wingspan: 46 cm

Cuckoos are slender birds with long tails that have large white spots on the underside. Two species occur in southern Ontario: the yellow-billed cuckoo and the black-billed cuckoo (*C. erythropthalmus*). Both lay larger clutches when outbreaks of cicadas or tent caterpillars provide an abundant food supply. • The yellow-billed cuckoo or "rain crow" has a propensity for calling on dark, cloudy days and a reputation for predicting rainstorms. **Where found:** semi-open deciduous woodlands; also dense riparian thickets, orchards, urban parks and abandoned farmlands; breeds south of Sudbury.

Eastern Screech-Owl

Megascops asio

Length: 20–23 cm
Wingspan: 51–56 cm

The diminutive eastern screech-owl is a year-round resident of low-elevation, deciduous woodlands. It survives even in our large cities by hunting in backyards and city parks at night and roosting quietly during the day in dense foliage or nest boxes. • Unique among Ontario owls, eastern screech-owls show both red and grey colour morphs. The red morph is less common here because it is less able to withstand our cold winters. **Where found:** mature deciduous forests, riparian areas, cities or orchards with shade trees; occurs from Algonquin Park south; also Sault Ste. Marie area.

Great Horned Owl

Bubo virginianus

Length: 46–64 cm
Wingspan: 91–152 cm

This highly adaptable and superbly camouflaged hunter has sharp hearing and powerful vision that allow it to hunt at night as well as by day. The leading edge of the flight feathers is fringed rather than smooth, which interrupts airflow over the wing and allows the owl to fly noiselessly. • Great horned owls begin their courtship as early as January, and by February and March, the females are already incubating their eggs. **Where found:** fields, open woodlands and wetlands; year-round resident throughout, except in the extreme north.

Snowy Owl

Bubo scandiacus

Length: 51–69 cm
Wingspan: 1.4–1.7 m (female is noticeably larger)

Feathered to the toes, the ghostly white snowy owl is well adapted to frigid winter temperatures. Its transparent feathers trap heat like a greenhouse, especially when ruffled out. • Male snowy owls will stockpile lemmings at nest sites for foggy or rainy days when hunting is poor. Nests have been found in the Arctic with up to 56 lemmings piled nearby. When lemming and vole populations crash in the Arctic, more Snowy Owls venture south to search for food. **Where found:** open country, including meadows and lakeshores; winter visitor throughout Ontario.

Northern Saw-whet Owl

Aegolius acadicus

Length: 18–23 cm
Wingspan: 43–55 cm

The tiny northern saw-whet owl makes the most of every hunting opportunity. When prey is abundant in winter, the saw-whet will catch extra food and store it in trees to freeze. When hunting efforts fail, the hungry owl returns to thaw out the frozen cache, "incubating" the food as if it were a clutch of eggs! • Listen for this small owl's evenly spaced, repeated whistle on spring nights. **Where found:** coniferous and mixed forests; wooded city parks and ravines; breeds in southern ½ of Ontario; winter resident from Ottawa south.

Common Nighthawk

Chordeiles minor

Length: 22–25 cm
Wingspan: 61 cm

You may know the common nighthawk from the male's dramatic aerial courtship display. He flies high overhead, uttering nasal *peent* notes, then dives with his wings extended. At the bottom of the dive, wind rushing through the primary feathers produces a hollow booming sound. • The nighthawk also feeds in midair. Its large, gaping mouth is surrounded by feather shafts that funnel insects into its bill. • When resting, this bird sits lengthwise on tree branches. **Where found:** open country, suburban and urban areas; often near water during migration; breeds and migrates throughout Ontario except the northern tundra.

Whip-poor-will

Caprimulgus vociferus

Length: 23–25 cm
Wingspan: 41–49 cm

These magical, elusive birds blend seamlessly into lichen-covered bark or the forest floor. On spring evenings, their airy, soothing *whip-poor-will* calls float through the open woodlands, and are attractive to prospective mates. • Ground-nesting whip-poor-wills time their egglaying to the lunar cycle so that hatchlings can be fed more efficiently during the light of the full moon. For the first 20 days after hatching, until the young are able to fly, the parents feed them regurgitated insects. **Where found:** open deciduous and pine woodlands; often along forest edges; breeds in southern ½ of Ontario.

Chimney Swift

Chaetura pelagica

Length: 11–14 cm
Wingspan: 30–32 cm

Chimney swifts are the "frequent fliers" of the bird world—they feed, drink, bathe, collect nest material and even mate while they fly! Watch for small flocks above cities and towns, catching insects at dusk. • During night migrations, swifts sleep as they fly, relying on changing wind conditions to steer them. Migrating chimney swifts may fly as high as 3000 m—above this altitude aircraft are required to carry oxygen. **Where found:** forages above cities and towns; roosts and nests in chimneys or occasionally tree cavities; breeds in southern ½ of Ontario.

Ruby-throated Hummingbird

Archilochus colubris

Length: 9.0–9.5 cm
Wingspan: 11.5 cm

Hummingbirds rank among the most interesting of birds, busily zooming in and out of our gardens and pollinating flowers in the process. Weighing about as much as a nickel, a hummingbird has a heart rate of over 1000 beats per minute, and its wings beat up to 60 times per second. They are the only birds capable of flying backwards. • Hummingbirds are attracted to the colour red, but do not add red food colouring to sugarwater feeders, because it may harm the birds. **Where found:** open, mixed woodlands, wetlands, flower gardens and backyards; breeds in the southern ½ of Ontario.

Belted Kingfisher

Ceryle alcyon

Length: 28–36 cm
Wingspan: 51 cm

Perched on a bare branch over a productive pool, the belted kingfisher will utter a scratchy, rattling call before plunging headfirst into the water to snatch a fish or a frog. Back on land, the kingfisher will flip its prey into the air and swallow it headfirst. • Mating pairs nest in a chamber at the end of a long tunnel dug into an earth bank. • With an extra red band across her belly, the female kingfisher is more colourful than her mate. **Where found:** lakes, ponds and rivers; breeds throughout Ontario; rarely overwinters in the south.

Red-headed Woodpecker

Melanerpes erythrocephalus

Length: 24 cm
Wingspan: 43 cm

This bird of the East lives mostly in open deciduous wood-lands, urban parks and oak savannahs. Red-heads were once common throughout their range, but their numbers have declined dramatically over the past century. Since the introduction of the European starling, red-headed woodpeckers have been largely out-competed for nesting cavities. **Where found:** open deciduous woodlands (especially oak woodlands), urban parks, river edges and roadsides with groves of scattered trees; breeds and rarely overwinters in southern Ontario.

Yellow-bellied Sapsucker

Sphyrapicus varius

Length: 18–20 cm
Wingspan: 41 cm

Parallel, horizontal rows of "wells" drilled into tree trunks indicate that sapsuckers are nearby. The sapsucker drills the wells, waits for them to fill with sweet, sticky sap and trap bugs, and then returns to lap up both with a tongue that resembles a paintbrush. A pair of sapsuckers may drill many sites within their territory. • Listen for yellow-bellied sapsuckers in May, when pairs tap in rhythmic duets. **Where found:** deciduous and mixed forests, especially dry, second-growth woodlands; breeder and migrant throughout Ontario, except in the north.

Downy Woodpecker

Picoides pubescens

Length: 15–18 cm
Wingspan: 31 cm

A bird feeder well stocked with peanut butter and black-oil sunflower seeds may attract a pair of downy woodpeckers to your backyard. These approachable little birds visit feeders more often than the larger, more aggressive hairy woodpeckers (*P. villosus*). Both downies and hairies have white outer tail feathers, but the downy's have several dark spots while the hairy's are pure white. • Woodpeckers have feathered nostrils, which filter out the sawdust produced by hammering. **Where found:** deciduous and mixed forests; year-round resident in southern ¾ of Ontario.

Northern Flicker

Colaptes auratus

Length: 32–33 cm
Wingspan: 51 cm

The northern flicker spends much of its time on the ground, feeding on ants. Flickers also clean themselves by squashing ants and preening themselves with the remains. Ants contain formic acid, which kills small parasites on the birds' skin and feathers. Flickers also bathe in dusty depressions. The dust particles absorb oils and bacteria that can harm the birds' feathers. • Flickers are named for their call, which sounds like *wicka-wicka-wicka*. **Where found:** open woodlands and forest edges, fields, meadows, beaver ponds and other wetlands; breeds throughout Ontario except on tundra.

Pileated Woodpecker

Dryocopus pileatus

Length: 41–48 cm
Wingspan: 74 cm

The pileated woodpecker, with its flaming red crest, chisel-like bill and commanding size, requires 40 hectares of mature forest as a home territory. • Foraging pileated woodpeckers leave large, rectangular cavities at the base of trees. A pair of woodpeckers will spend up to 6 weeks excavating a large nest cavity in a dead or decaying tree. Wood ducks, kestrels, owls and even flying squirrels nest in abandoned cavities. **Where found:** mature forests, riparian woodlands and occasionally suburban woodlots or agricultural areas; year-round resident in the southern ⅔ of Ontario.

Olive-sided Flycatcher

Contopus cooperi

Length: 19 cm
Wingspan: 30 cm

The olive-sided flycatcher's upright, attentive posture contrasts with its comical song: *quick-three-beers! quick-three-beers!* Like a dutiful parent, this flycatcher changes its tune during nesting, when it more often produces an equally enthusiastic *pip-pip-pip.* • Olive-sided flycatchers nest high in the forest canopy. Far above the forest floor, they have easy access to an abundance of flying insects, including honeybees and adult wood-boring and bark beetles. **Where found:** open coniferous and mixed forests, wetlands, burned areas; breeds throughout Ontario except on tundra.

Eastern Phoebe

Sayornis phoebe

Length: 15–18 cm
Wingspan: 27 cm

Whether you are poking around a barnyard, a campground picnic shelter or your backyard shed, there is a very good chance you will stumble upon an eastern phoebe family and their marvellous mud nest. Once limited to nesting on natural cliffs and fallen riparian trees, this adaptive flycatcher has found success nesting in culverts and under bridges and eaves, especially near water. **Where found:** open deciduous woodlands, forest edges and clearings; breeds in the southern ½ of Ontario.

Great Crested Flycatcher

Myiarchus crinitus

Length: 20–23 cm
Wingspan: 30 cm

Loud, raucous *wheep!* calls and bright yellow and rufous feathers give away the presence of the great crested flycatcher. Unlike other eastern flycatchers, the great crested prefers to nest in a tree cavity or abandoned woodpecker hole, or sometimes uses a nest box intended for a bluebird. Occasionally, the nest entrance will be decorated with a shed snakeskin or translucent plastic wrap. The purpose of this practice is not fully understood. **Where found:** deciduous and mixed woodland edges and clearings; breeds in the southern ½ of Ontario.

Eastern Kingbird

Tyrannus tyrannus

Length: 22 cm
Wingspan: 38 cm

The eastern kingbird lives up to its scientific name,
Tyrannus tyrannus. It will fearlessly attack crows,
hawks and even humans that pass through its
territory, pursuing and pecking at them until
the threat has passed. The eastern kingbird
is a gregarious fruit eater while wintering in
South America, and an antisocial, aggressive insect eater while nesting in North
America. **Where found:** fields, forest clearings, shrubby roadsides, towns and
farmyards; breeds throughout the southern ⅔ of Ontario.

Northern Shrike

Lanius excubitor

Length: 25 cm
Wingspan: 37 cm

One of the most vicious predators in the bird world,
the northern shrike relies on its sharp, hooked bill
to catch and kill small birds or rodents, which
it spots from treetop perches. Its tendency
to impale its prey on thorns and barbs for
later consumption has earned it the name "butcher bird." • Northern Shrikes
visit our region each winter in unpredictable and highly variable numbers.
Where found: *Breeding:* sparse coniferous woodlands and muskeg of northern
Ontario. *In migration* and *winter:* open country, farmyards, towns and roadsides
throughout the province.

Red-eyed Vireo

Vireo olivaceus

Length: 15 cm
Wingspan: 25 cm

Capable of delivering about 40 phrases per minute, the male
red-eyed vireo can out-sing any one of his courting neighbours. One particularly vigorous male holds the record
for the most songs—about 22,000!—delivered by a single bird in a single day. • This bird is hard to spot
because it forages high in the canopy, where its dull
colours offer camouflage. It perches with a hunched
stance and hops with its body turned diagonally to its direction of travel. **Where found:**
deciduous or mixed woodlands; breeds throughout Ontario except on tundra.

Gray Jay

Perisoreus canadensis

Length: 28–33 cm
Wingspan: 46 cm

These curious, fearless birds won't hesitate to follow you in their search for tasty morsels. Often unusually bold in campgrounds and parking lots, these crafty creatures may steal your lunch right from under your nose! They are known to hide bits of food under the bark of trees, to be retrieved in times of need. • Unlike most mountain birds, gray jays build their nests and raise their young in late winter or early spring. **Where found:** coniferous forests; year-round resident throughout Ontario, except in the extreme north. **Also known as:** Canada jay, whiskey jack.

Blue Jay

Cyanocitta cristata

Length: 28–31 cm
Wingspan: 41 cm

This loud, striking bird is well known throughout our province. Blue jays can be quite aggressive when competing for sunflower seeds and peanuts at backyard feeding stations and rarely hesitate to drive away smaller birds, squirrels or even threatening cats. Even the great horned owl is not too formidable a predator for a group of these brave, boisterous mobsters to harass. **Where found:** mixed forests, agricultural areas, scrubby fields and townsites; breeds in the southern ⅔ of Ontario; overwinters in the southern ⅓ of the province.

American Crow

Corvus brachyrhynchos

Length: 43–53 cm
Wingspan: 94 cm

The noise that most often emanates from this treetop squawker seems unrepresentative of its intelligence. However, this wary, clever bird is also an impressive mimic, able to whine like a dog and laugh or cry like a human. • Crows will drop walnuts or clams from great heights onto a hard surface to crack the shells, one of the few examples of birds using objects to manipulate food. As ecological generalists, crows can survive in a wide variety of habitats and conditions. **Where found:** urban areas, agricultural fields and marshes; breeds throughout Ontario, except on tundra; overwinters in southern Ontario.

Common Raven

Corvus corax

Length: 61 cm
Wingspan: 1.3 m

Glorified in native cultures throughout the Northern Hemisphere, the
common raven doesn't act by instinct alone.
From producing complex vocalizations to
playfully sliding down snowbanks, this raucous bird exhibits behaviours that
many people once thought of as exclusively human. • When working as a pair to
confiscate a meal, one raven may act as the decoy while the other steals the food.
Where found: coniferous and mixed forests and woodlands; townsites, campgrounds and landfills; year-round resident throughout Ontario except in the
extreme south.

Horned Lark

Eremophila alpestris

Length: 18 cm
Wingspan: 30 cm

Performing an impressive, high-speed, plum-
meting courtship dive would blow back any-
body's hair, or in the case of the horned lark, its
2 unique black "horns." • This bird's tinkling song will be one of the first you hear
introducing spring. • Horned larks are often abundant at roadsides, searching for
seeds, but an approaching vehicle usually sends them flying into an adjacent field.
Where found: open areas, including pastures, native prairie, cultivated fields, golf
courses and tundra; breeds in southern and northern Ontario; common migrant
throughout; rare winter visitor in the extreme south.

Purple Martin

Progne subis

Length: 18–20 cm
Wingspan: 46 cm

These large swallows will entertain you throughout
spring and summer in return for you setting up luxurious "condo complexes" for them. Purple martins
once nested in natural tree hollows and in cliff crevices
but now have virtually abandoned these in favour of
human-made housing. To avoid the invasion of aggressive
house sparrows or European starlings, it is essential for
martin condos to be cleaned out and closed up after each nesting season. **Where
found:** semi-open areas, often near water; breeds in the southern ⅓ of Ontario.

Tree Swallow

Tachycineta bicolour

Length: 14 cm
Wingspan: 37 cm

Tree swallows are often seen perched beside their fencepost nest boxes. When conditions are favourable, these busy birds are known to return to their young 10–20 times per hour (about 140–300 times a day!). • In the evening and during light rains, small groups of foraging tree swallows sail gracefully above rivers and wetlands, catching stoneflies, mayflies and caddisflies. **Where found:** open woodlands, fencelines with bluebird nest boxes, backyards and wetlands; often near water; breeds throughout Ontario.

Barn Swallow

Hirundo rustica

Length: 18 cm
Wingspan: 38 cm

Beautiful barn swallows have a distinctive, deeply forked tail. • They once nested on cliffs, but are now found more frequently nesting on barns, boathouses and under bridges and house eaves. Their nests are constructed by rolling mud into small balls, one mouthful of mud at a time. A swallow's nest built on your house is a sign of good luck in many cultures. **Where found:** rural and urban areas; often near water; common breeder throughout Ontario.

Black-capped Chickadee

Poecile atricapillus

Length: 13–15 cm
Wingspan: 20 cm

The black-capped chickadee is one of the most common and approachable songbirds in Ontario. Its cheerful calls and sunny, curious disposition make it a welcome visitor on morning walks and at backyard feeders. • Chickadees are omnivorous cavity nesters that usually lay 6–8 eggs in late winter or early spring. • Small flocks of foraging birds can often be seen swinging upside-down on tree branches, snatching up insects or berries. On cold winter nights, chickadees may huddle together in the shelter of tree cavities or other suitable hollows. **Where found:** mixed and deciduous forests, parks and suburban backyards; year-round resident throughout Ontario, except in the extreme north.

Red-breasted Nuthatch

Sitta canadensis

Length: 11 cm
Wingspan: 22 cm

The red-breasted nuthatch has a somewhat dizzying view of the world. This interesting bird, with its distinctive black eye line and red breast, moves down tree trunks headfirst, cleaning up the seeds, insects and nuts that woodpeckers may have overlooked. • Nuthatches are an irruptive species, more common in some winters than others, but populations appear to be increasing throughout their range. They are attracted to backyard bird feeders filled with suet or peanut butter. **Where found:** coniferous and mixed forests; breeds in the southern ⅔ of Ontario; overwinters in the southern ⅓.

White-breasted Nuthatch

Sitta carolinensis

Length: 15 cm
Wingspan: 28 cm

This bird is commonly seen and heard year round in riparian areas, along forest edges, in parks and throughout urban areas with many large deciduous trees. In summer, it specializes in finding and eating insects and spiders. Its ability to walk headfirst down the trunks of trees gives it a unique perspective, allowing it to find insect eggs and pupae that most birds miss. During winter visits to bird feeders, this bird can be seen flying off to hide the seeds in crevices under the bark of trees. **Where found:** deciduous and mixed forests; year-round resident in the southern ⅓ of Ontario.

House Wren

Troglodytes aedon

Length: 12 cm
Wingspan: 15 cm

Boisterous and energetic, the curious house wren is a familiar bird in suburban yards and parks. It is readily identified by its lovely bubbling song and short tail, which is often held straight up. • The house wren will apparently nest in any cavity or enclosed space, including woodpecker holes, flowerpots, boots, drain pipes and even parked cars! **Where found:** thickets and shrubby openings, often near buildings; deciduous or mixed woodland edges; breeds in the southern ½ of Ontario.

Marsh Wren

Length: 13 cm
Wingspan: 15 cm

The reclusive marsh wren breeds deep within cattail marshes. This bird's distinctive song, a rapid series of gurgling notes followed by a trill, is reminiscent of an old-fashioned sewing machine. • The male marsh wren is polygynous and may mate with 2 or more females. For each female he is courting, he typically builds at least 6 "dummy" nests and takes his potential mate on a tour to inspect them. **Where found:** cattail marshes; breeds in Lake of the Woods area and south of Sudbury.

Ruby-crowned Kinglet

Regulus calendula

Length: 10 cm
Wingspan: 19 cm

The male ruby-crowned kinglet's familiar, complex, warbling song echoes through our boreal forests in spring and summer. Unfortunately, his distinctive crown is only visible in breeding season, leaving him with just his dull olive green plumage for the rest of the year. • Female kinglets can lay an impressively large clutch with up to 12 eggs, which together often weigh as much as the bird that laid them! **Where found:** mixed and coniferous forests, especially with spruce; breeds throughout Ontario; rare winter visitor in the south.

Eastern Bluebird

Sialia sialis

Length: 18 cm
Wingspan: 33 cm

The eastern bluebird's enticing colours are like those of a warm setting sun against a deep blue sky. In earlier decades, the removal of standing dead trees and nesting competition with house sparrows and European starlings, both introduced species, reduced some bluebird populations. The establishment of "trails" of bluebird nest boxes on fence posts along highways and rural roads has aided in the recovery of this species. **Where found:** agricultural lands and fencelines, meadows, forest clearings and edges, large lawns; breeds throughout the southern ½ of Ontario; rarely overwinters in the south.

Hermit Thrush

Catharus guttatus

Length: 18 cm
Wingspan: 29 cm

The hermit thrush's haunting, flute-like song may be
one of the most beautiful natural melodies. Similar
to the song of the Swainson's thrush (*C. ustulatus*),
the song of the hermit thrush is almost always
preceded by a single questioning note. • This thrush feeds mainly on
insects, worms and snails during the summer, but adds a wide variety
of fruit to its winter diet. • When alarmed, the hermit thrush flicks its wings,
raises its tail, and utters harsh *chuck* notes. **Where found:** most brushy or wooded
habitats with leaf litter, especially near water; breeds throughout Ontario.

American Robin

Turdus migratorius

Length: 25 cm
Wingspan: 43 cm

Come March, the familiar song of
the American robin may
wake you early if you are a
light sleeper. This abundant
bird adapts easily to urban areas
and often works from dawn until after dusk when there is a nest to be built or
hungry young mouths to feed. In autumn, fruit trees may attract flocks of robins,
which gather to drink the fermenting fruit's intoxicating juices. **Where found:**
residential lawns and gardens, urban parks, broken forests, bogs and river shorelines; breeds throughout Ontario, except on tundra; rarely overwinters in the
south.

Gray Catbird

Dumetella carolinensis

Length: 22–23 cm
Wingspan: 28 cm

The gray catbird is an accomplished mimic that may fool
you as it shuffles through underbrush and dense riparian
shrubs, calling its cat-like meow. Its mimicking talents are further
enhanced by its ability to sing 2 notes at once, using each side of its
syrinx individually. The gray catbird will vigilantly defend its territory
against sparrows, robins, cowbirds and other intruders, even destroying the eggs
and nestlings of other songbirds. **Where found:** dense thickets, brambles or shrubby
areas and hedgerows, often near water; breeds in the southern ½ of Ontario.

Brown Thrasher

Toxostoma rufum

Length: 29 cm
Wingspan: 33 cm

The brown thrasher has the streaked breast of a thrush and the long tail of a catbird, but it has a temper all its own. Because it nests close to the ground, the thrasher defends its nest with a vengeance, attacking snakes and other nest robbers sometimes to the point of drawing blood. • Biologists have estimated that the male brown thrasher is capable of producing up to 3000 distinctive song phrases—the most extensive vocal repertoire of any North American bird. **Where found:** dense thickets and woodland edges; breeds in the southern ½ of Ontario.

European Starling

Sturnus vulgaris

Length: 22 cm
Wingspan: 41 cm

The European starling was intentionally introduced to North America. About 100 birds were released in New York's Central Park in 1890 and 1891, as part of a plan to release into the U.S. all of the birds mentioned in Shakespeare's works. This highly adaptable bird took over the nest sites of native cavity nesters and learned to mimic the sounds of many birds. Today, about 200 million starlings are believed to occupy the continent. **Where found:** cities, towns, farmyards, woodland fringes and clearings; year-round resident in the southern ½ of Ontario.

Cedar Waxwing

Bombycilla cedrorum

Length: 18 cm
Wingspan: 30 cm

With its black mask and slick hairdo, the cedar waxwing has a heroic look. This bird's splendid personality is reflected in its amusing antics after it gorges on fermented berries and in its gentle courtship dance. A courting male hops toward a female and offers her a berry. The female accepts the berry and hops away, then stops and hops back toward the male to offer him the berry in return. **Where found:** wooded residential parks and gardens, overgrown fields, riparian areas; breeds throughout Ontario; replaced in winter by the Bohemian waxwing (*B. garrulus*).

Yellow Warbler

Dendroica petechia

Length: 13 cm
Wingspan: 20 cm

The widely distributed yellow warbler arrives in May, singing its *sweet-sweet* song. It is often mistakenly called a "wild canary" because of its bright plumage.
• This warbler is often parasitized by the brown-headed cowbird and can recognize cowbird eggs, but rather than tossing them out, it will build another nest overtop the old eggs or abandon the nest completely. Occasionally, cowbirds strike repeatedly—a five-storey nest was once found! **Where found:** habitat generalist; moist, open woodlands, scrubby meadows, urban parks and gardens; breeds throughout Ontario.

Yellow-rumped Warbler

Dendroica coronata

Length: 13–15 cm
Wingspan: 23 cm

Yellow-rumped warblers are the most abundant and widespread wood-warblers in North America. This small warbler's habit of flitting near buildings to snatch spiders from their webs has earned it the nickname "spider bird." • This species comes in 2 forms: the common, white-throated "myrtle warbler" of the East, and the yellow-throated "Audubon's warbler" of the West. • Small puddles that form during or after rains often attract warblers, allowing a glimpse of these secretive birds. **Where found:** mature coniferous and mixed woodlands; breeds throughout Ontario.

American Redstart

Setophaga ruticilla

Length: 13 cm
Wingspan: 20 cm

Known as "butterfly bird" in some parts of its range, the American redstart rarely, if ever, sits still. In its seemingly nonstop pursuit of prey, this bird flushes insects with a flash of colour from its wings or tail. Then it uses its broad bill and rictal bristles (the short, whisker-like feathers around its mouth) to capture insects like an expert flycatcher. • Its Latin American name, *candelita,* means "little torch." **Where found:** deciduous woodlands and shrubby woodland edges; often near water; breeds in the southern ⅔ of Ontario.

Ovenbird

Seiurus aurocapilla

Length: 15 cm
Wingspan: 24 cm

In summer, the male's loud *tea-cher* song will give away his presence as he hides among tangled shrubs or conifer branches, but even the sharpest human eye will have trouble spotting the ovenbird's immaculately concealed nest. The unusual Dutch oven–shaped ground nest is so well camouflaged that incubating females will choose to sit tight rather than flee in the presence of danger. Unfortunately, forest fragmentation and brown-headed cowbird parasitism have reduced this bird's nesting success. **Where found:** undisturbed, mature forests with little understorey; breeds throughout boreal forest areas and southern Ontario.

Common Yellowthroat

Geothlypis trichas

Length: 11–14 cm
Wingspan: 18 cm

The bumblebee colours of the male common yellowthroat's black mask and yellow throat identify this skulking wetland resident. He sings his *witchety* song from strategically chosen cattail perches that he visits in rotation, fiercely guarding his territory against the intrusion of other males. The female lacks a mask and usually remains hidden from view in thick vegetation. • Unlike most wood-warblers, the common yellowthroat prefers marshlands and wet, overgrown meadows to forests. **Where found:** wetlands, riparian areas and wet, overgrown meadows; breeds throughout boreal forest areas and southern Ontario.

Scarlet Tanager

Piranga olivacea

Length: 17–19 cm
Wingspan: 29 cm

Despite the vibrant red of the breeding male scarlet tanager, birders tend to hear this canopy dweller before they see it. Its song is a slurred version of the American robin's. • Watch for scarlet tanagers during cold, rainy weather, when they forage in the forest understorey and are easier to observe. • The scarlet tanager has the northernmost breeding grounds and longest migration route of all tanager species. **Where found:** dense, mature forest; breeds in the southern ½ of Ontario.

Chipping Sparrow

Spizella passerina

Length: 13–15 cm
Wingspan: 22 cm

The chipping sparrow usually sings from a high perch but commonly nests at eye level. You can even take part in this bird's nest-building activities by leaving samples of your pet's hair—or your own—around your backyard. • This bird's trilling song is very similar to that of the dark-eyed junco. Listen for a slightly faster, drier and less musical series of notes to identify the chipping sparrow. **Where found:** open conifers or mixed woodland edges, shrubby yards and gardens; breeds throughout Ontario except in the northeast corner.

Song Sparrow

Melospiza melodia

Length: 14–18 cm
Wingspan: 21 cm

The well-named song sparrow is among the great singers of the bird world. When a young male is only a few months old, he has already created a courtship tune of his own, having learned the basics of melody and rhythm from his father and rival males. • Mild winters and a well-stocked feeder sometimes convince a few of these songsters to overwinter in southern Ontario. **Where found:** shrublands, riparian thickets, forest openings and pastures, often near water; breeds throughout Ontario.

White-throated Sparrow

Zonotrichia albicollis

Length: 17–18 cm
Wingspan: 23 cm

The white-throated sparrow's distinctive *oh sweet Canada Canada Canada* song makes it one of the easiest sparrows to learn and identify. Its familiar bold, white throat and striped crown can only be confused with the white-crowned sparrow (*Z. leucophrys*), but white-throats usually stick to forested woodlands, whereas white-crowns prefer open, bushy habitats and farmlands. • Two colour morphs are common: one has black and white stripes on the head; the other has brown and tan stripes. **Where found:** coniferous and mixed forests; breeds throughout Ontario.

Dark-eyed Junco

Junco hyemalis

Length: 14–17 cm
Wingspan: 23 cm

Juncos usually congregate in backyards with bird feeders and sheltering conifers—with such amenities at their disposal, more and more juncos are appearing in urban areas. They spend most of their time on the ground, snatching up seeds, and they are readily flushed from wooded trails and backyard feeders. Their distinctive, white outer tail feathers flash in alarm as they seek cover in a nearby tree or shrub. • Five closely related subspecies occur in North America. **Where found:** shrubby woodland borders, backyard feeders; breeds throughout Ontario; overwinters in the southern ⅓ of Ontario.

Northern Cardinal

Cardinalis cardinalis

Length: 19–23 cm
Wingspan: 30 cm

A male northern cardinal will display his unforgettable, vibrant red head crest and raise his tail when he is excited or agitated. He will vigorously defend his territory, even attacking his own reflection in a window or hubcap! • Cardinals are one of only a few bird species to maintain strong pair bonds. Some couples sing to each other year round, while others join loose flocks, reestablishing pair bonds in spring during a "courtship feeding." A male will offer a seed to the female, which she then accepts and eats. **Where found:** woodland edges, thickets, backyards and parks; year-round resident in the southern ⅓ of Ontario.

Rose-breasted Grosbeak

Pheucticus ludovicianus

Length: 18–21 cm
Wingspan: 32 cm

Whistling its unhurried tune, the rose-breasted grosbeak sounds like a robin that has taken singing lessons. Although the female lacks the magnificent colours of the male, she shares his talent for beautiful song. • Rose-breasted grosbeaks usually build their nests low in a tree or tall shrub. By contrast, they typically forage high in the canopy where they can be difficult to spot. The abundance of berries in fall often draws these birds to ground level. **Where found:** deciduous and mixed forests; breeds in the southern ½ of Ontario.

Indigo Bunting

Passerina cyanea

Length: 14 cm
Wingspan: 20 cm

The vivid electric blue male indigo bunting is one of the most spectacular birds in Ontario. These birds arrive in April or May and favour raspberry thickets as nest sites. Dense, thorny stems keep most predators at a distance and the berries are a good food source. • The male bunting is a persistent singer, vocalizing even through the heat of a summer day. • Planting coneflowers, cosmos or foxtail grasses may attract indigo buntings to your backyard. **Where found:** deciduous forest and woodland edges, orchards and shrubby fields; breeds in the southern ⅓ of Ontario.

Bobolink

Dolichonyx oryzivorus

Length: 15–20 cm
Wingspan: 29 cm

Originally a prairie species, the bobolink benefited from the clearing of the eastern deciduous forests and expanded its range eastward to exploit new habitats. • A vociferous male bobolink may defend and mate with several females, but he does not stay for long after the young have hatched. • The bobolink is the most migratory blackbird, and makes a round-trip voyage of up to 20,000 km from its northern breeding grounds to Brazil or Argentina and back again. **Where found:** tall, grassy meadows and ditches, hayfields and croplands; breeds in the southern ½ of Ontario.

Red-winged Blackbird

Agelaius phoeniceus

Length: 18–24 cm
Wingspan: 33 cm

The male red-winged blackbird wears his bright red shoulders like armour—together with his short, raspy song, they are key in defending his territory from rivals. In field experiments, males whose red shoulders were painted black soon lost their territories. • These birds are early spring arrivals, often returning to Ontario in late March. Numerous pairs may nest in an area, filling wetlands with their loud, raspy *konk-a-ree* or *ogle-reeeee* calls. **Where found:** cattail marshes, wet meadows and ditches, croplands and shoreline shrubs; breeds throughout boreal forest areas and south; overwinters in southern Ontario.

Eastern Meadowlark

Sturnella magna

Length: 23–24 cm
Wingspan: 36 cm

The drab dress of most female songbirds lends them protection during the breeding season, but the female eastern meadowlark uses a different strategy. Her V-shaped "necklace" and bright yellow throat and belly create a colourful distraction that leads predators away from the nest. A female flushed from the nest while incubating her eggs will often abandon the nest, but she will never abandon her chicks. **Where found:** grassy meadows and pastures, weedy fields and old orchards; breeds in the southern ⅓ of Ontario.

Brown-headed Cowbird

Molothrus ater

Length: 15–20 cm
Wingspan: 30 cm

These nomads historically followed bison herds across the Great Plains (they now follow cattle), so they never stayed in one area long enough to build and tend a nest. Instead, cowbirds lay their eggs in other birds' nests, relying on the unsuspecting adoptive parents to incubate the eggs and feed the aggressive young. Increased livestock farming and fragmentation of forests has encouraged the expansion of the cowbird's range. It is known to parasitize more than 140 bird species. **Where found:** agricultural and residential areas, woodland edges; breeds in the southern ½ of Ontario.

Baltimore Oriole

Icterus galbula

Length: 18–20 cm
Wingspan: 29 cm

With its flute-like song and a preference for the canopies of neighbourhood trees, the Baltimore oriole is easier to hear than see. A hanging pouch nest dangling in a bare tree in autumn is sometimes the only evidence that the bird was there at all. The nests are deceptively strong and often remain intact through the harshest winters. **Where found:** open deciduous and mixed forests, particularly riparian woodlands; breeds in the southern ½ of Ontario.

Purple Finch

Carpodacus purpureus

Length: 13–15 cm
Wingspan: 25 cm

Despite this bird's name, the purple finch's stunning plumage is more of a raspberry red than a shade of purple. • The male finch often delivers his musical warble from an exposed perch at the top of a live tree. A flat, raised, table-style feeding station and nearby tree cover are sure to attract purple finches and erecting a feeder may keep a small flock in your area over winter. **Where found:** coniferous and mixed forests; breeds throughout boreal forest areas and south; rare winter visitor in southern Ontario.

Common Redpoll

Carduelis flammea

Length: 13 cm
Wingspan: 23 cm

Redpolls sometimes make only a modest appearance, showing up in winter in small groups. Other winters, dozens flock together, gleaning waste grain from bare fields or stocking up at winter feeders. • A large surface area relative to a small internal volume puts the common redpoll at risk of freezing in low temperatures. A high intake of food and the insulating layer of warm air trapped by its fluffed feathers keep this songbird from dying of hypothermia. **Where found:** *Breeding:* shrubby tundra and boreal taiga of northern Ontario. *In migration* and *winter:* weedy fields, roadsides and backyard feeders throughout the province.

American Goldfinch

Carduelis tristis

Length: 11–14 cm
Wingspan: 23 cm

Like vibrant rays of sunshine, American goldfinches cheerily flutter over weedy fields, gardens and along roadsides. It is hard to miss their jubilant *po-ta-to-chip* call and their distinctive, undulating flight style. • These acrobatic birds regularly feed while hanging upside down. Finch feeders are designed with the seed openings below the perches to discourage the more aggressive, upright-feeding birds. Use niger or black-oil sunflower seeds to attract American goldfinches to your bird feeder. **Where found:** weedy fields, riparian areas, parks and gardens; breeds in the southern ½ of Ontario; overwinters from the Algonquin Park area south.

House Sparrow

Passer domesticus

Length: 14–17 cm
Wingspan: 24 cm

A black mask and bib adorn the male of this adaptive, aggressive species. These well-known birds frequent fast-food restaurant parking lots, backyard bird feeders and farms. • This abundant and conspicuous bird was introduced to North America in the 1850s as part of a plan to control the insects that were damaging grain and cereal crops. As it turns out, these birds are largely vegetarian and usually feed on seeds and grain! **Where found:** any human environment; year-round resident in southern ⅔ of Ontario.

AMPHIBIANS & REPTILES

Amphibians and reptiles are commonly referred to as cold-blooded, but this is misleading. Although amphibians and reptiles lack the ability to generate their internal body heat, they are not necessarily cold-blooded. These animals are ectothermic or poikilothermic, meaning that the temperature of the surrounding environment governs their body temperature. The animal will obtain heat from sunlight, warm rocks and logs, and warmed earth. Amphibians and reptiles hibernate in winter in cold regions, and some species of reptiles estivate in summer in hot regions. Both amphibians and reptiles moult (shed their skins) as they grow to larger body sizes.

Amphibians are smooth-skinned and most live in moist habitats. They are represented by the salamanders, frogs and toads. They typically lay shell-less eggs in jelly-like masses in water. These eggs hatch into gilled larvae (larvae of frogs and toads are called tadpoles), which then metamorphose into adults with lungs and legs. Amphibians can regenerate their skin and often even entire limbs. Male and female amphibians often differ in size and colour, and males may have other diagnostics when sexually mature, such as the vocal sacs in many frogs and toads.

Reptiles are fully terrestrial vertebrates with scaly skin. In this guide, the representatives are turtles, lizards and snakes. Most reptiles lay eggs buried in loose soil, but some snakes and lizards give birth to live young. Reptiles do not have a larval stage.

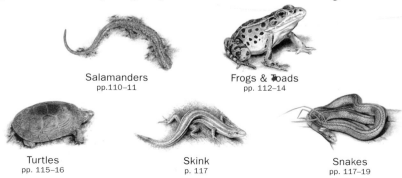

Salamanders
pp.110–11

Frogs & Toads
pp. 112–14

Turtles
pp. 115–16

Skink
p. 117

Snakes
pp. 117–19

Mudpuppy

Necturus maculosus

Length: 48 cm

Mudpuppies are large, deep-water salamanders that spend their entire lives in the water. Unlike other salamanders, mudpuppies keep their feathery external gills throughout their adult lives. • These bottom dwellers spend much of their time eating aquatic insects, crayfish and small fish or hiding under debris on the bottom of lakes and streams. Unless accidentally caught on a fish hook they are seldom seen. **Where found:** year round at bottoms of rivers and lakes; south of Kenora, Thunder Bay, Sault Ste. Marie and North Bay.

Eastern Newt

Notophthalmus viridescens

Length: *Adult:* 14 cm; *Eft:* 4–8 cm.

Eastern Newts have 3 life stages: they begin life in the water as tadpoles, spend 1–3 years on land as juveniles or efts, and then return to the water as adults. • The vivid, bright orange colour of efts warns predators against their toxicity. Look for efts on rainy evenings in moist, forested habitats. • Adult newts are yellowish green with 2 rows of red spots outlined in black. **Where found:** efts prefer moist forests; adults favour slow-moving, weedy water; south of Lake of the Woods, Lake Nipigon and Timmins.

Spotted Salamander

Ambystoma maculatum

Length: 20 cm

Like all mole salamanders, this secretive amphibian spends most of its time buried beneath the forest floor, eating earthworms, insects and other invertebrates. The best time to see a spotted salamander is on a rainy spring night, when groups gather in clear, shallow ponds to breed. Females lay jelly-like clumps of up to 300 eggs, which are attached to underwater vegetation. • The spotted salamander may live for over 30 years. There are 4 species of mole salamanders in Ontario. **Where found:** forested regions near wetlands; hibernates underground in winter; east from Thunder Bay and Lake Nipigon to Timmins and south.

Northern Two-lined Salamander

Eurycea bislineata

Length: 12 cm

Lungless salamanders have neither gills nor lungs, but instead absorb oxygen through their moist skin and mouth lining. To avoid drying out the salamander's skin and suffo-cating it, the best way to observe this amphibian is in a water-filled, clear plastic bag. To identify a northern two-lined salamander, look for 2 dark lines running down the adult's yellow or golden back. Ontario's 4 lungless salamander species are slightly larger, slimmer and have shorter legs than mole salamanders. **Where found:** prefers fast-moving streams; forages in adjacent woodlands in summer; hibernates under streambeds during winter; southeast of Timmins and Algonquin Park.

Four-toed Salamander

Hemidactylium scutatum

Length: 10 cm

Unlike other Ontario salamanders, the four-toed salamander is usually found in sphagnum bogs. It has only 4 toes on its hind feet (except for the mudpuppy, other Ontario species have 5 toes) and a unique white belly that is covered with black spots. The tail base is constricted, marking the place where the tail would break away if bitten by a predator. **Where found:** sphagnum bogs and occasionally moist forests; hibernates under soil in winter; from Sudbury and North Bay south, excluding heavily populated areas.

Eastern Red-backed Salamander

Plethodon cinereus

Length: 10 cm

Although eastern red-backed salamanders are plentiful, they spend much of their time hiding under leaf litter and are rarely seen. Two variable colour forms occur here: the typical red-backed form and a less common lead-backed (grey) form. Some red-backs have black dots or a black line running down the centre of their backs. • This salamander catches aphids, worms and other small invertebrates by thrusting out its sticky tongue. **Where found:** moist, forested areas; hibernate communally in underground burrows during winter; north shore Lake Superior east to Timmins/Kirkland Lake and south.

American Toad

Bufo americanus

Length: 11 cm

The most memorable way to meet American toads is to visit a breeding pond in mid-April or early May. For a few days each spring, groups of these explosive breeders gather in shallow wetlands to mate, summoned by the loud chorus of trilling males. They depart just as suddenly, leaving long strings of eggs along the bottoms of ponds. • Thick skin that minimizes water loss allows the American toad to occupy relatively dry habitats. Each wart on the skin contains a white poison to deter predators. **Where found:** various habitats including forests, meadows, suburban backyards and gardens; hibernates under soil in winter; throughout Ontario except in the extreme north.

Grey Treefrog

Hyla versicolor

Length: 6 cm

Five treefrogs occur in Ontario, but not all spend time in trees. Climbing species such as the grey treefrog have larger sticky discs at the ends of their toes than ground-dwelling species. • Juvenile grey treefrogs are an eye-catching bright green but change to a camouflage grey colour as adults. Sexes can be distinguished by throat colour: dark on males and white on females. • Treefrogs breed in weedy ponds, depositing clumps of floating eggs. **Where found:** woodlands near water; hibernates under soil or leaves; south of Kenora, Thunder Bay, Sault Ste. Marie and North Bay.

Spring Peeper

Pseudacris crucifer

Length: 3.5 cm

The high-pitched *peep* of this small frog signals the arrival of spring. In southern Ontario, breeding begins as early as March, typically in shallow ponds that are not yet ice-free. Tadpoles spend about 3 months in the pond before transforming to frogs and dispersing into the forest. • These treefrogs spend much of their time buried in the leaf litter on the ground. Spring peepers are easily identified by the dark, X-shaped mark on their tan to grey backs. They have white undersides. **Where found:** forest floor near water; hibernate under leaf litter in winter; southern ⅔ of Ontario.

Western Chorus Frog

Pseudacris triseriata

Length: 3 cm

In early spring, chorus frogs can be heard calling from wetlands, ditches and sloughs across much of Canada. This common sound—much like someone running a finger down the teeth of a comb—is often heard with the *cluck cluck* of wood frogs. • Two chorus frogs are found in Ontario: the western chorus frog of the south and the similar-looking boreal chorus frog (*P. maculata*) north and west of Wawa. Both of these tiny frogs have a grey-brown body, a dark eye stripe and 3 darker stripes (sometimes broken) running along their backs.
Where found: breeds in ponds and ephemeral water bodies; winters under leaf litter; south of Algonquin Park.

American Bullfrog

Rana catesbeiana

Length: 20 cm

Big and hungry, the bullfrog consumes whatever it can wrap its mouth around, including ducklings, small birds, insects, fish and other frogs. In turn, they fall prey to birds, snakes and mammals—including humans, who consider this frog's legs a delicacy. • Although females lay large, floating mats of 8000–25,000 eggs, bullfrog numbers are decreasing as overharvesting, habit loss and habitat degradation take their toll. • True to its name, the bullfrog sounds like a grunting bull.
Where found: large, permanent water bodies with cover; overwinters underwater; south of the North Bay area.

Green Frog

Rana clamitans

Length: 10 cm

Like the stereotypical frog, green frogs are typically found in ponds full of lily pads. • Large green frogs sit motionless before diving into the water, unlike similar-looking mink frogs and bullfrogs, which skip across surface vegetation before plunging in. Look for the folds or ridges along the green frog's back and dark bars on its hind legs. The bullfrog lacks these ridges but has a ridge circling the tympanum, and the mink frog has dark blotches on its hind legs. • The male green frog's call is a single, banjo-like twang. **Where found:** adults in or near permanent water; overwinters underwater; southern ½ of Ontario.

Northern Leopard Frog

Rana pipiens

Length: 11 cm

Green with dark spots—that's the pattern of the northern leopard frog. One of the most widespread frog species in Canada, you may have also encountered this frog during the dissection unit of a biology class. In the 1970s, this widespread frog underwent mysterious, localized extinctions. Most eastern populations have recovered, but western populations, especially in BC, have not. Since amphibians are sensitive to environmental conditions and are indicators of a healthy environment, unexplained extinctions are alarming. **Where found:** in summer in meadows and fields; overwinters on lake bottoms; throughout Ontario except in the extreme north.

Mink Frog

Rana septentrionalis

Length: 7.5 cm

If you are handling a frog that smells like a mink (something like rotting onions), you've caught a mink frog. This frog prefers ponds full of lily pads to use for hunting, cover and escape. Try searching for the mink frog after dark, because it will usually sit motionless under a flashlight beam. • The male's raspy *tuk tuk tuk* breeding call is heard in spring. **Where found:** adults in or near permanent water with abundant lily pads or vegetation; southern ⅔ of Ontario.

Wood Frog

Rana sylvatica

Length: 6.5 cm

Wood frogs are fascinating because they can freeze. At below-zero temperatures, their heart rate, blood flow and breathing stop, turning them into froggy ice cubes. Special antifreeze, mainly glucose, allows wood frogs to survive to −6°C and occur north of the Arctic Circle. These frogs jump farther than other frogs and may also be more intelligent because they creep toward prey. • The croak of a male wood frog sounds suspiciously similar to a mallard duck's quack, so don't be fooled in spring. **Where found:** moist woodlands, often far from water; throughout Ontario.

Common Snapping Turtle

Chelydra serpentina

Length: 45 cm

Strong jaws, a long tail and an algae-covered shell give the snapping turtle a prehistoric look. • This turtle spends most of its time underwater, walking along the lake or pond bottom, eating weeds and scavenging for carrion. It rarely basks, though the female travels over land to lay up to 40 white, spherical eggs (our other turtles lay oval eggs). • Snapping turtles are aggressive on land and may try to bite. **Where found:** large lakes, occasionally smaller water bodies; from Lake of the Woods area to Thunder Bay and from Lake Nipissing area south.

Stinkpot

Sternotherus odoratus

Length: 13 cm

Our other algae-covered turtle, the stinkpot, has an oval, domed shell and gives off a skunk-like odour when distressed. This small turtle inhabits still, shallow water bodies, walking along the bottom in search of aquatic invertebrates and carrion or basking at the water's surface. • Once widespread in southern Ontario, stinkpot populations are declining because of shoreline development and collisions with boat propellers. They are now listed as a threatened species in Ontario and Canada. **Where found:** Georgian Bay and from the Pembrook area south. **Also known as:** musk turtle.

Spiny Softshell Turtle

Apalone spinifera

Length: 42 cm

Also known as the "pancake turtle," this large turtle has a soft, leathery shell. • The spiny softshell turtle ambushes prey by burying itself in the mud or lying in wait in the shallows, using its tubular snout to breathe. It feeds on molluscs, fish and crustaceans. Look for softshells basking near the shore on sandbars or logs. • Softshell populations are threatened in Ontario because of habitat loss or degradation from agricultural activity, shoreline development, accidental commercial fishery catches and pollution. **Where found:** large lakes and rivers; Pembrooke area and exteme southwestern Ontario.

115

Painted Turtle

Chrysemys picta

Length: *Midland:* 15 cm; *Western:* 25 cm

Painted turtles can often be seen basking in the sun on top of floating logs, mats of vegetation or exposed rocks. When alarmed, they slip into the water for a quick escape. • These turtles may live up to 40 years. • Two subspecies are common in Ontario. The midland painted turtle has a dark green or black carapace (shell) with yellow, orange or red underside borders. The larger western painted turtle has an olive green carapace with red or orange underside borders. **Where found:** marshes, ponds, lakes and slow-flowing streams. *Midland:* southeastern ⅓ of Ontario. *Western:* north and west of Lake Superior.

Blanding's Turtle

Emydoidea blandingi

Length: 20 cm

A high-domed shell makes the Blanding's turtle a poor swimmer. It prefers to walk along the pond bottom, feeding on aquatic invertebrates and vegetation. • Like all pond turtles, the Blanding's turtle can pull its head and limbs into its shell when threatened. The flexible plastron (underside covering) moves to partially seal the shell. The plastron is flat or convex in females and concave in males. **Where found:** edges of shallow water bodies, in areas with thick weeds; from Lake Nipissing south.

Northern Map Turtle

Graptemys geographica

Length: *Female:* 27 cm; *Male:* 13 cm

Fine, pale lines give this turtle's shell the look of a topographical map. • Although groups of northern map turtles are frequently seen basking on rocks or logs, close-up glimpses are usually brief, because the turtles dive when alarmed. • These excellent swimmers may travel long distances, especially to communal hibernation sites. Females are much larger and use their strong jaws to crush shellfish, their main food source. Males are smaller and feed on aquatic insects or crayfish. **Where found:** large lakes and rivers; south of Lake Nipissing.

Common Five-lined Skink

Eumeces fasciatus

Length: 20 cm

The common five-lined skink is
our only member of the lizard
family. This quick, secretive
reptile basks in the sun during the day
or darts about under rocks, logs or leaf
litter, feeding on invertebrates. • Juveniles have a blue tail, but the colour fades in
adulthood. Like many other lizards, it may shed its tail to escape when restrained.
• In Ontario, skink populations are declining because of shoreline development
and poaching for the pet trade. **Where found:** most common in wooded habitats with
ground cover; between Lake Nipissing and Lake of Bays; also south of London.

Common Gartersnake

Thamnophis sirtalis

Length: 60 cm (maximum 100 cm)

Swift on land and in water, the
common gartersnake is an
efficient hunter of amphibians,
fish, small mammals, slugs and
leeches. • Hundreds of gartersnakes will overwinter together in an underground
hibernaculum, emerging each spring to mate, then disperse. A single female can
give birth to 3–83 live young in a single litter. • The colour and pattern of these
familiar snakes varies greatly. The base colour is dark olive green to black, and
stripes, or occasionally checkers, may be yellow, orange, red or brown. **Where
found:** meadows, suburban or urban areas, sometimes near water; throughout the
southern ⅔ of Ontario.

DeKay's Brownsnake

Storeria dekayi

Length: 52 cm

Small DeKay's brownsnakes often live
in towns and cities, but they may be
hard to find. They like to burrow into
leaf litter, where their small size and brown
colour offers camouflage, or hide under flat rocks and
boards. Snails, slugs and earthworms are their main food items.
• Snakes smell with their tongues, collecting scents from the air and then
interpreting them using a special organ located in their mouths. **Where found:**
various habitats including suburban and urban sites; hides under objects; from
the Lake Nipissing area south.

Red-bellied Snake

Storeria occipitomaculata

Length: 40 cm

Distinguished by a red to pink-coloured belly and keeled scales, this snake is easy to identify but may be hard to find. Red-bellied snakes usually remain hidden under fallen logs, rocks or leaf litter. Your best chance of meeting one is on a rainy or overcast night, when these snakes emerge to feed on small invertebrates, especially slugs. Females bear up 12 live young in the fall. During winter, groups hibernate in a den. **Where found:** forest floor, under cover; southern ½ of Ontario.

Smooth Greensnake

Opheodrys vernalis

Length: 65 cm

The colouration of this diurnal snake gives it superb camouflage among grasses, herbs and shrubs, but after death, its colour quickly changes to bluish grey. • A number of female smooth greensnakes may share a single nesting site, where each female lays 3–12 eggs under rocks, in loose soil. If you are lucky, you may find some of these lovely snakes sheltered under logs, rocks or boards. Groups often hibernate in anthills. **Where found:** moist meadows, rocky areas, forests and riparian areas; south of the Timmins area.

Ring-necked Snake

Diadophis punctatus

Length: 60 cm

Smooth scales, a bluish grey back, yellow underside and a distinct yellow neck-band are the trademarks of the adult ring-necked snake. Although young DeKay's brownsnakes and red-bellied snakes have similar neckbands, their scales are keeled and their underside colouration differs. • Eastern red-backed salamanders make up the bulk of the ring-necked snake's diet. • Occasionally, a ringneck may end up in your basement. These harmless reptiles release a musky odour when handled. **Where found:** moist woodlands; southern ⅓ of Ontario.

Northern Watersnake

Nerodia sipedon

Length: 135 cm

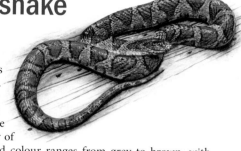

Often found near water, these curious
snakes sometimes approach swimmers.
Although watersnakes are neither
aggressive nor venomous, they will
bite, defecate or spray if handled. • These
thick-bodied snakes come in a variety of
colours and patterns. The background colour ranges from grey to brown, with
darker bands near the head, followed by alternating back and side blotches. • Prey
includes small vertebrates such as frogs and fish, as well as invertebrates. **Where
found:** near or in water; hibernates underground; southern ⅓ of Ontario.

Milksnake

Lampropeltis triangulum

Length: 90 cm

Although milksnakes can be
common on farms, these snakes do
not milk cows, as folklore suggests.
Rather, these constrictors prey on the mice
and rats that are attracted to barns or old buildings. They also eat frogs, bird eggs and
invertebrates. • This aggressive snake will bite when handled and shake the tip
of its tail like a rattlesnake when threatened. • To identify a milksnake, look for
a pale "Y" or "V" marking on the head and the bold pattern. **Where found:** forests,
meadows, edge habitats, agricultural areas; throughout the southern ⅓ of Ontario.

Massasauga

Sistrurus catenatus

Length: 100 cm

Our only venomous snake, the
massasauga, has a rattle on the tip
of its tail and a distinctive black
belly. Like all pit vipers, it will lie
motionless, then suddenly strike, immobilizing
its prey (mainly rodents) with a venomous bite. When not in use, its fangs fold
backward. • These snakes usually retreat before they are noticed. Few bites have
been reported in Ontario and only one death. The poison is slow acting, but
all victims should be hospitalized. **Where found:** dry, upland areas in summer;
forested wetlands in spring and fall; hibernates singly in winter; Bruce Peninsula,
Georgian Bay area, isolated populations in southwestern Ontario.

FISH

F ish are ectothermic vertebrates that live in the water, have streamlined bodies covered in scales, and possess fins and gills. A fundamental feature of fish is the serially repeated set of vertebrae and segmented muscles that allow the animal to move from side to side, propelling it through the water. A varying number of fins (depending on the species) further aid the fish to swim and navigate. Most fish are oviparous and lay eggs that are fertilized externally. Eggs are either produced in vast quantities and scattered, or they are laid in a spawning nest (redd) under rocks or logs. Parental care may be present in the defence of such a nest or territory. Spawning can involve migrating vast distances back to freshwater spawning grounds after spending 2–3 years in the ocean.

Lamprey & Sturgeon
p. 122

Carp & Shiner
pp. 122–23

Sucker
p. 123

Catfish & Pike
pp. 123–24

Smelt
p. 124

Salmon & Trout
pp. 124–26

Burbot
p. 126

Stickleback
p. 127

Sculpin
p. 127

Bass, Perch & Drum
pp. 127–29

Freshwater Eel
p. 129

Goby
p. 129

Sea Lamprey

Petromyzon marinus

Length: *Ammocetes:* 10 cm (maximum 15 cm);
Adults: 53–76 cm

Lampreys are usually anadromous and return to fresh water only to spawn, but Ontario's sea lampreys have adapted to fresh water. With the building of the Welland Canal in 1829, lampreys gained access to the Great Lakes, arriving in the ballast water of marine vessels. They were first noted in Lake Erie in 1921, and then quickly and explosively invaded the entire Great Lakes system, resulting in reductions of native benthic feeders and various commercial fishery stocks. • Sea lampreys spend much of their lives as benthic ammocetes (larvae), sucking up plankton and algae. After 4–6 years, the parasitic adults emerge, latching onto larger fish with their powerful, jawless mouths and feeding on the host fish's blood and bodily fluids. **Where found:** Great Lakes and St. Lawrence Seaway. *Ammocetes:* bottom sediment of rivers or tributaries. *Adults:* large lakes and rivers.

Lake Sturgeon

Acipenser fulvescens

Length: 0.75–1.43 m (occasionally over 2 m)

For 100 million years, the lake sturgeon has nosed along river bottoms, using the 4 barbels that surround its mouth to detect prey. This scaleless relic has 5 rows of hard plates called "scutes" running down its body. • Unfortunately, this formerly abundant species is now threatened because of overharvesting of eggs for caviar, overfishing and habitat degradation. • Lake sturgeon can live up to 80 years, and individuals once grew to over 2 m in length, making it Ontario's largest freshwater fish. **Where found:** large lakes and rivers throughout the province. **Also known as:** black sturgeon, rock fish, bony sturgeon.

Common Carp

Cyprinus carpio

Length: 38–46 cm (maximum 102 cm)

Our largest minnow, the common carp, thrives throughout much of North America in eutrophic lakes, irrigation ditches and even sewage outlets. This omnivorous fish roots along the bottom for food, uprooting and sucking in aquatic vegetation, then expelling it back into the water to separate edible items. These destructive feeding habits increase turbidity and destroy spawning, rearing and feeding grounds important for native fish and wildlife. **Where found:** silty, organically rich lakes; warm, weedy, fairly shallow waters; southern Ontario, spreading northward. **Also known as:** carp, scaled carp, mirror carp, leather carp.

Emerald Shiner

Notropis atherinoides

Length: 5–7.5 cm (maximum 12 cm)

This common baitfish is abundant in our larger rivers and lakes and important to many predators, both aquatic and avian. Emerald shiner populations fluctuate greatly, influencing the populations of many fish in the process. • These minnows spend much of their time in open water feeding on plankton, which they follow up to the surface at dusk. You may see these little jewels in autumn, when large schools gather near shorelines and docks. • The related creek chub (*Semotilus atromaculatus*) is our most common stream minnow. **Where found:** open water of lakes and large rivers; shallow lakeshores in spring and autumn; southern ⅔ of Ontario. **Also known as:** lake shiner, common shiner, buckeye shiner.

White Sucker

Catostomus commersoni

Length: 25–41 cm (maximum 61 cm)

The white sucker is a generalist species that lives in various habitats, ranging from cold streams to warm, even polluted, waters. It avoids rapid currents and uses shallow areas to feed. During the spring spawning season, you may see mating white suckers splashing and jostling next to streams or shallow lakeshores. The suckers migrate upstream shortly after the ice breaks up, providing an important food source for other fish, eagles and bears. Once hatched, the fry are also a critical forage item for other young fish. **Where found:** variable habitats; prefers cool, clean waters with sandy or gravel substrate; throughout Ontario. **Also known as:** common sucker, mud sucker, brook sucker.

Channel Catfish

Ictalurus punctatus

Length: 37–53 cm (maximum 1.3 m)

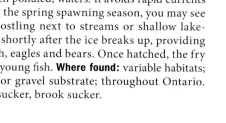

The channel catfish is the largest and most sought-after member of the catfish family in Canadian waters. • This slender fish has small eyes and a long, wide head, but its characteristics change considerably with size, sex, season and geographic location. • The species name *punctatus* means "spotted" in Latin and refers to the spots that cover most of the channel catfish's body, though fish over 30 cm long often do not have spots. **Where found:** cool, clear, deep water; sometimes found in brackish water or lakes; also larger rivers; southwestern Ontario, Lake of the Woods area. **Also known as:** channel cat, spotted catfish, northern catfish, lake catfish.

Northern Pike

Esox lucius

Length: 46–76 cm (maximum 133 cm; female is larger than male)

If you canoe, watch for adult pike hanging motionless among the reeds or along the edges of a dense aquatic plant bed. This carnivorous fish hunts by lying in wait, then ambushing its prey, which may be other fish, ducklings or shorebirds. It attacks with a quick stab of its long snout, clamping down on its victim with heavily toothed jaws. • The muskellunge (*E. masquinongy*) or "muskie" is the largest member of the pike family in Ontario. It is found in the Great Lakes region. **Where found:** vegetated edges of warmer lakes and rivers; throughout Ontario. **Also known as:** jackfish, pickerel, water wolf.

Rainbow Smelt

Osmerus mordax

Length: 18–23 cm

Originally introduced to the Great Lakes in the early 1900s as a forage fish for salmonids, the rainbow smelt actually feeds on young fish. Smelt have proven to be a threat to salmonids and other native fish. In addition to small fish, smelt eat crustaceans and occasionally aquatic and terrestrial insects. • In 1948, a commercial smelt fishery began in the Great Lakes and soon grew to exceed the Atlantic Coast fishery in both weight and market value. A year-round sport fishery is also active. **Where found:** cool, deep, offshore waters; Ottawa River, St. Lawrence Seaway, Great Lakes and tributaries. **Also known as:** American smelt.

Chinook Salmon

Oncorhynchus tshawytsch

Length: 30–100 cm (landlocked fish)

As the largest Pacific salmon, the chinook has rightfully earned the nickname "king salmon" by tipping the scales at a whopping 57 kg. That's heavier than most supermodels! Only wild chinook in the Pacific Ocean reach this large size; Ontario's landlocked specimens remain much smaller, usually less than 9 kg. • In 1872, the chinook became the first Pacific salmon to be stocked around the world. For many years, the only self-sustaining, anadromous population to survive was on New Zealand's South Island. • The Atlantic salmon (*Salmo salar*) was extirpated from Lake Ontario and is now being reintroduced. **Where found:** stocked in the Great Lakes. **Also known as:** king salmon, tyee, spring salmon.

Rainbow Trout

Oncorhynchus mykiss

Length: 30–46 cm (maximum 91.5 cm)

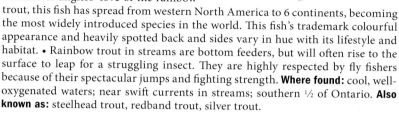

Because of anglers' love of the rainbow trout, this fish has spread from western North America to 6 continents, becoming the most widely introduced species in the world. This fish's trademark colourful appearance and heavily spotted back and sides vary in hue with its lifestyle and habitat. • Rainbow trout in streams are bottom feeders, but will often rise to the surface to leap for a struggling insect. They are highly respected by fly fishers because of their spectacular jumps and fighting strength. **Where found:** cool, well-oxygenated waters; near swift currents in streams; southern ½ of Ontario. **Also known as:** steelhead trout, redband trout, silver trout.

Brown Trout

Salmo trutta

Length: 25–40 cm (maximum 87 cm)

The "brownie" has been so much a part of European heritage that early settlers introduced "their" fish to North America and many other regions of the world. Many of the fish were either von Behr trout from Germany or Loch Leven trout from Scotland. Today, the populations are mixed and indistinguishable. • Brownies are drift feeders, with preference for streams with cover and an intermediate water flow. They can handle warmer water temperatures and higher turbidity than other members of the trout family, so may be introduced to streams disturbed by logging or industrial activity. **Where found:** various water bodies, lakes; mainly in the southern ⅓ of Ontario. **Also known as:** German brown trout, English brown trout, brownie.

Brook Trout

Salvelinus fontinalis

Length: 15–25 cm (maximum 86 cm)

The unique patterns of the brook trout make it hard to confuse with any other species. The vermiculations, or "worm tracks," on their backs set these handsome fish apart from other Ontario fish. • The brook trout is actually a char, distinguishable by the "jelly doughnuts" (red or yellow dots with blue halos) on its sides. Another fish with "jelly doughnuts," the brown trout, is a true trout and has a light body with black spots. • Native to eastern North America, brook trout were the pioneers of fish introduction and have spread widely. **Where found:** cold, clear, slow-moving waters; clear shallow areas of lakes; throughout Ontario, absent west of Lake Nipigon. **Also known as:** speckled trout, spotted trout, brook char.

Lake Trout

Salvelinus namaycush

Length: 45–65 cm (maximum 125 cm)

Large, solitary lake trout prefer ice-cold water. In summer, they follow the retreat of colder water to the bottom of a lake, rarely making excursions into the warm surface layer. • Despite their slow growth, lake trout can reach old ages and large sizes. Large trout can be often over 20 years old, with one granddaddy of a specimen reaching 62 years old! • Lake trout can take 6 years or more to reach maturity and may spawn only once every 2–3 years, making recovery from overfishing difficult. • They are native to Ontario. **Where found:** usually in deep, cooler lakes; southern ⅔ of Ontario. **Also known as:** laker, Great Lakes trout.

Lake Whitefish

Coregonus clupeaformis

Length: 40 cm (maximum 63 cm)

Lake whitefish are what biologists call a "plastic species," which means that they change their behaviour, food habits and appearance in different habitats. One of the best identifiers for different forms is the number of gillrakers. Fish that live in more open water develop extended gillrakers that are better for filtering plankton. Lake whitefish caught closer to the surface tend to have higher gillraker counts than those that nibble food from the lake bottom. • The lake whitefish and cisco (*C. artedii*) are Ontario's most common and widespread whitefish. **Where found:** cool, deep water at the bottom of larger lakes; occasionally in rivers; throughout Ontario. **Also known as:** humpback whitefish, eastern whitefish, Great Lakes whitefish.

Burbot

Lota lota

Length: 30–80 cm (maximum 1.0 m)

The burbot is the only member of the cod family confined to fresh water. • The single chin barbel and the pectoral fins contain taste buds. As these fish grow, they satisfy their ravenous appetite for whitefish and suckers by eating larger fish instead of more smaller ones, sometimes swallowing fish almost as big as themselves. A 30-cm-long walleye was once found in the stomach of a large burbot. • Once considered by anglers to be a "trash" fish, the burbot is gaining popularity among sport fishers. **Where found:** bottom of cold lakes and rivers; throughout Ontario. **Also known as:** freshwater cod, eelpout, ling, lawyer, loche.

Brook Stickleback

Culaea inconstans

Length: 5 cm (maximum 8.7 cm)

This common, plentiful
little fish is distinguished by
4–6 spines that run along its back. It is one of
the easiest fish to see and can be found along the edges of water bodies that have
plenty of vegetation. • Brook sticklebacks are tolerant of low oxygen levels and can
live in waters where other fish cannot, even spreading into flooded farmers' fields that
may eventually leave them high and dry. **Where found:** varied; ponds, saline sloughs,
rivers, creeks, lake edges; aquatic vegetation is required for breeding; throughout
Ontario. **Also known as:** black stickleback, five-spined stickleback, pinfish.

Mottled Sculpin

Cottus bairdi

Length: 7.6 cm (maximum 13 cm)

Female mottled sculpins literally
fall "head over tail" in love. After
entering the male's burrow, the female turns upside down to
deposit her sticky eggs on the underside of the rock or ledge that covers the den.
Topsy-turvy females must also be tactical, because cannibalistic males will swallow small females. Once she has released her eggs, the swollen-headed male drives
her off, intent on attracting other mates to his burrow. With a view box to elimi-
nate surface riffles, you may be lucky enough to spot a mottled sculpin on the nest.
Where found: bottom dweller; usually in cool, clean streams and lakes with rocky
substrate; throughout Ontario. **Also known as:** bullhead, blob, miller's thumb.

Smallmouth Bass

Micropterus dolomieu

Length: 20–30 cm (maximum 68.6 cm)

Often sought by anglers, both
smallmouth and largemouth
bass (*M. salmoides*) are native to east-central
North America. • Spawning males return to almost the exact
same nesting spot each year and aggressively guard their nests, sometimes even
driving females away. Females must be extremely persistent to gain access to the
nest. When the male finally accepts her, the pair remains in the nest for almost
2 hours, releasing eggs and sperm about every 30 seconds. **Where found:** lakes,
reservoirs and streams with rocky or sandy bottoms; southern ½ of Ontario.
Also known as: smallmouth black bass, brown bass.

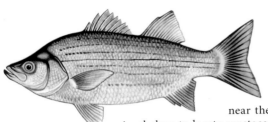

White Bass

Morone chrysops

Length: 20–30 cm

You may see schools of these important game fish feeding near the surface. These native fish use visual clues to locate crustaceans, smaller fish or other prey. • In spring, schools separate into sex-specific groups and return to spawn in the streams where they were hatched. • The related white perch (*M. americana*) invaded the Great Lakes through the Welland and Erie Canals, and may be responsible for declines of native fish populations, including walleye and white bass. **Where found:** clear water and rocky reefs in the lower Great Lakes and St. Lawrence River. **Also known as:** silver bass, white lake-bass, striped bass.

Pumpkinseed

Lepomis gibbosus

Length: 15–20 cm (maximum 23 cm)

The pumpkinseed is a schooling fish that may be seen swimming through the sunny shallows in large numbers. Their gold-flecked bodies reflect the sunlight, so these fish appear to shimmer as they move. • Native to the Atlantic drainages of east-central North America, the pumpkinseed has been widely introduced elsewhere. • Since pumpkinseeds are small fish, they are ideal forage food for other predatory fishes such as bass, walleye or yellow perch. **Where found:** clear, shallow lakes; slow-moving waters; usually near cover such as submerged logs or weeds; southern ½ of Ontario, except Lake Superior. **Also known as:** common sunfish, sun bass, yellow-belly, yellow sunfish.

Walleye

Stizostedion vitreum

Length: 40–60 cm (maximum 90 cm)

A popular game fish among Ontario anglers, the walleye is a piscivorous fish prized for its tasty flesh and sporting qualities. • It has black and gold flecks all over its body and 2 dorsal fins. The first dorsal fin is spiny, the second is fleshy. • In "two-storey" lakes, brown trout inhabit the cool bottom depths, while walleye stick to the warmer "top floor"—the surface waters and shallows. **Where found:** large rivers and relatively deep lakes; prefers low amounts of light; throughout Ontario. **Also known as:** pickerel, pike-perch, wall-eyed pike.

Freshwater Drum

Aplodinotus grunniens

Length: 40–50 cm

The large freshwater drum is occasionally encountered but not often recognized. In turbid waters, they are silver-coloured, but in clearer waters they appear bronze. This fish is easily identified by its 2 dorsal fins: a spiny front fin joined to a soft posterior fin by a small membrane. • Mature males develop specialized muscles that vibrate against their swim bladders to produce odd, grunting noises, giving rise to the species name *grunniens*, meaning "grunting." **Where found:** large water bodies with a sandy bottom, mainly in the lower Great Lakes. **Also known as:** croaker, grinder, grunt, sheepshead, thunder pumper.

American Eel

Anguilla rostrata

Length: 30–91 cm (maximum 152 cm)

Historically, American eels found their way up the St. Lawrence Seaway to Lake Ontario, but the construction of the Welland Canal has likely allowed them occasional access to Lake Erie and beyond. Mature eels swim 6000 km from Lake Ontario downstream to the Sargasso Sea in the Atlantic Ocean, where they spawn and likely die. Larvae drift with the Gulf Stream, eventually changing into young eels and making their way back to the coastal streams of eastern North America, a long journey that takes a year or more. **Where found:** Ottawa River, St. Lawrence Seaway, Lake Ontario and tributaries; occasionally in Lakes Erie, Huron and Superior.

Round Goby

Neogobius melanostomus

Length: 25 cm

Although gobies have a worldwide distribution, these fish were not found in the Great Lakes until 1995. They were likely introduced via the ballast water of marine vessels and have undergone rapid expansions in both population and range. These voracious bottom feeders have well-developed sensory organs that allow them to feed in darkness and outcompete native benthic species. Gobies are also extremely aggressive at spawning sites, limiting the access of native fish. • Unlike similar-looking sculpins, gobies have a fused pelvic fin. **Where found:** Lakes Michigan, Erie, Huron and Superior.

INVERTEBRATES

More than 95% of all animal species on the planet are invertebrates, and there are thousands of invertebrate species in Ontario. The few mentioned in this guide are frequently encountered and easily recognizable. Invertebrates can be found in a variety of habitats and are an important part of most eco-systems. They provide food for birds, amphibians, shrews, bats and other insects, and they also play an important role in the pollination of plants and aid in the decay process.

Aquatic Invertebrates
pp. 131–32

Grovesnail
p. 132

Butterflies & Moths
pp. 133–34

Dragonfly
p. 135

Beetles
p. 135

Cicada
p. 136

Mosquitoes
p. 136

Ants, Wasps & Bees
pp. 136–37

Non-Insect Arthropods
pp. 137–38

Caddisfly Larvae

Pycnopsyche spp.

Length: with case, up to 60 mm.

Here are larvae worth looking for! These tiny
architects build a protective casing or shell around
their soft bodies by gluing together sand, twigs or
leaves using saliva and silk. The tube-shaped or coiled casings act as camouflage.
• Search for caddisfly larvae on the bottom of shallow ponds or small creeks.
Watch for pieces of moving debris with eyes and wiggly legs at one end. The larvae
become moth-like adults with long, wispy antennae and are an important food
source for fish. **Where found:** ponds, lakes, rivers and streams.

Zebra Mussel

Dreissena polymorpha

Length: about 15 mm

Since their discovery in 1988 in Lake St. Clair, these invasive
molluscs have spread rapidly through the Great Lakes, the
St. Lawrence River and into some tributaries and lakes.
They are nearly invisible in their early larval life stage, and
can be transported unintentionally in ballast water or bait
buckets. Adults attach to boats, anchors or boat trailers.
These mussels have a high reproduction rate and are a serious pest, colonizing intake pipes and restricting flow to water treatment
plants and altering spawning reefs of native and sport fish. • Our native freshwater mussel, the spike (*Elliptio dilatata*), is dark brown and much larger, up to
12.7 cm in length. **Where found:** freshwater lakes.

Mayflies

Hexagenia spp.

Length: 20–30 mm.

Mayflies develop for several years as aquatic larvae, then
moult twice within hours to emerge as adults. The short-
lived adults lack feeding mouthparts and survive on land for
only one day, swarming together to mate. Males die soon after
mating, but the females drop back down to the water, where they
lay their eggs before perishing. Anglers celebrate these spectacular hatches
because they attract feeding trout to the surface. Amazingly, mayfly hatches have
been linked to the bloom time of specific flowering plants, which vary annually
with changes in temperature and light. The seasonal rhythm of lifecycle events, in
this case the connection between insects, flowers and fish, falls under a branch of
science known as phenology. **Where found:** near water.

Virile Crayfish

Orconectes virilis

Length: 10–12 cm

This smaller, freshwater relative of the lobster spends most daylight hours under rocks, logs or other shelter, hiding from predators. • Virile crayfish have a brown or rusty red, shell-like carapace, 2 long antennae and a pair of large, often bluish-tinted chelipeds (pincers). They feed on anything they can catch, including aquatic plants, invertebrates, tadpoles and small fish. • Virile crayfish are native from Alberta to Québec and into the northern United States but have been introduced farther south. They are used as bait and as food for humans and predacious aquarium fishes. **Where found:** bottom of lakes, rivers, streams, wetlands. **Also known as:** northern crayfish.

Water Strider

Gerris buenoi

Length: about 13 mm

This unique bug lives on the water's surface, relying on surface tension and 4 long, water-repellent legs to keep afloat. The water strider's legs distribute its body weight over the water's surface and allow it to zing about at up to 1.5 metres per second, leaving rings of water in its wake. • This sucking bug uses its 2 short, front legs to catch larvae or other insects that fall into the water. In turn, water striders are eaten by fish or birds. **Where found:** ponds, lakes, slow-moving streams. **Also known as:** pond skater.

Grovesnail

Cepaea nemoralis

Width: 25 mm

Colourfully banded grovesnails are common land snails, introduced to Ontario from Europe. There are many combinations of banding and shell colour, including white, yellow, pinkish and different shades of brown. Shell colour may be linked to the animal's body temperature, with dark shells absorbing more heat and occurring more often in shaded forests. Pale shells that reflect heat and reduce moisture loss appear to be more common in open areas such as grasslands. **Where found:** variety of habitats from grasslands to forests.

Cabbage White

Pieris rapae

Wingspan: 50 mm.

Every gardener is familiar with the cabbage white, an introduced butterfly whose caterpillars mercilessly bore little holes into garden vegetables. You will usually find cabbage whites fluttering about in sunny areas, because butterflies are unable to fly when cold.
• Common in both urban and agricultural habitats, the cabbage white is a good butterfly to take a closer look at. Its dark wing bases help to soak up sunlight, and the heat is then transferred to flight muscles. When the butterfly rests with its wings held slightly open, the white wing surface reflects light inward to heat the body. **Where found:** gardens and agricultural fields.

Eastern Tiger Swallowtail

Papilio glaucus

Wingspan: about 80 mm.

Large and brightly coloured, the eastern tiger swallowtail rarely goes unnoticed. It has a strong, elegant flight pattern and a distinctive way of fluttering its wings as it feeds on flower nectar. If you can sneak up to a swallowtail feeding at a flower, look for the long, black proboscis, the tube-like mouthpart that butterflies use for sucking up nectar. • As summer progresses, swallowtails mate and lay eggs, which hatch into smooth, leaf-green-coloured caterpillars. The cryptic caterpillars are decorated with 2 large eyespots midway down their bodies and may be found feeding on various trees and shrubs, especially poplars, chokecherries and willows. **Where found:** clearings, gardens and parks.

Spring Azure

Celastrina ladon

Wingspan: 25 mm

As spring arrives in Ontario, the tiny spring azure can be seen fluttering along the forest floor before the last snows have melted. With brilliant blue upper wings, males appear like tiny flowers come to life. They may be seen patrolling sheltered areas in search of their dull brown mates, and they are often found near red-osier dogwood or buffaloberry bushes. • Spring azures belong to a family of butterflies commonly known as "blues." **Where found:** common in forest clearings.

Mourning Cloak

Nymphalis antiopa

Wingspan: 70 mm.

You may be surprised to see a mourning cloak on a sunny day in April when patches of snow still cover the earth. These "early" butterflies are adults that have spent the winter under a piece of bark or within a woodpile and are often among the first butterflies to emerge in spring. • Most mourning cloaks begin their adult lives in July and feed on sap for a short time before becoming temporarily dormant until autumn. As the days become shorter, they become active again, feeding and seeking shelter for the winter. Adults hibernate until spring, emerge to mate, and then the females lay eggs that hatch in summer. Adult mourning cloaks can live almost one year, a record lifespan among butterflies. **Where found:** widespread in forested areas.

Monarch

Danaus plexippus

Wingspan: about 95 mm.

Large and beautiful, monarchs are famous for the amazing long-distance migration they undergo each year. In early summer, monarchs return from their wintering grounds in the mountains of central Mexico. It takes 2 generations to make the trip, so we see the grandchildren of the butterflies that began the long journey from Mexico. • As caterpillars, monarchs eat milkweed leaves and absorb a chemical that is toxic to birds. The monarch's bright orange-and-black pattern also serves to warn away predators. **Where found:** fields and meadows where milkweeds grow.

Luna Moth

Actias luna

Wingspan: about 95 mm

There are many moth species in Ontario, and not all are small and brown. The beautiful luna moth, with its light green wings and furry, white body, is our most elegant moth. • Green wings allow the luna moth to blend in perfectly with the leaves of birch trees. The "tails" on the hind wings lure predator bats toward the moth's hind end, rather than the head end, allowing the moth to escape relatively unscathed. • Luna moths are common but may be difficult to find, because they usually fly at night, and adults have a short lifespan of only about one week. **Where found:** deciduous forests; southern ½ of Ontario.

Common Green Darner

Anax junius

Length: up to 8 cm

Agile and deadly hunters of the air, dragon-flies are a hiker's best friend. In addition to providing awe-inspiring aerial shows and flashes of brilliant colour, these insects eat tremendous numbers of irritating biting insects, such as mosquitoes and black flies. Both the aquatic larvae and the aerial adult dragonflies possess voracious appetites. • Many dragonfly species can be easily identified by their colour-ful markings. Green darners have a green thorax and a bright blue abdomen. These dragonflies migrate with the warm weather and are common and widespread throughout North America. **Where found:** near ponds and lakes.

Firefly

Photurus pennsylvanicus

Length: about 12 mm.

When the summer moon casts its reflection on shimmering waters and gentle ripples lap Ontario's rocky shores, only the fire-flies' blinking lanterns can complete the magic. At night, courting fireflies spark their bright, yellowish green lights to attract mates. • A firefly is able to light up the tip of its abdomen using a reversible chemical reaction that is controlled by its brain. • Fireflies belong to the beetle family and hatch from eggs as larvae. The larvae also glow and are known as "glow worms." **Where found:** deciduous forests.

Multicoloured Asian Ladybug

Harmonia axyridis

Length: 5 mm

Ladybugs are some of our most familiar, well-loved insects. Not all are orange with black spots—species vary in size, colour and number of spots. • Multicoloured Asian ladybugs were released in Washington, Delaware and Georgia during the 1920s to control aphids that were devouring crops. They quickly spread along both coasts and inland and are now the most common species in Ontario. These ladybugs usually have a 10-spot pattern on an orange back, but black and unmarked forms also occur. • The name "ladybug" refers to the Lady Virgin Mary's red robes. **Where found:** throughout Ontario.

Dog-day Cicada

Tibicen canicularis

Length: 30 mm

Cicada hatches can be quite spectacular in some regions, but in Ontario you are more likely to hear them rather than see them. Males rest on tree branches and "sing" their buzzy, whiny song to females. The noise is produced by a vibrating membrane in the cicada's abdomen. • Cicadas have lifecycles of 2–5 years, but most of this time is spent as larvae that live underground and eat roots. Adults emerge in late summer and live for about 2 months. **Where found:** wooded areas.

Mosquitoes

Order Diptera

Length: 0.3–1.3 cm

The mosquito's buzzing is all too familiar, whether the sound is made by hundreds gathered outside your window screen or by a solitary fiend that has hidden in your bedroom until lights-out. The high-pitched sound is produced by the mosquito's wings, which beat up to 600 times per second and allow this tiny insect to sometimes travel as far as 160 km. • Of the over 2500 different mosquito species found worldwide, about 55 are found in Ontario. Only a small fraction of Ontario's mosquito species carry the deadly West Nile virus, and these tend to occur together, in specific areas or pools. **Where found:** throughout Ontario.

Carpenter Ant

Camponotus pennsylvanicus

Length: 10–15 mm

Ants represent one of the world's most successful faunal groups. Many species live in the Ontario, but carpenter ants are the biggest. • Carpenter ants use their strong jaws to chew through wood, but they are not termites. To spot a carpenter ant nest, look for piles of sawdust near a tree trunk or inside old wooden buildings. • Ant colonies have one large, egg-producing queen, many sterile workers and a few fertile, winged males and females that fly to new areas to mate and form new colonies. **Where found:** varied habitats from forests to urban areas.

Yellow Jackets

Vespula **spp.**

Length: 10–15 mm

Yellow jackets, also called wasps or hornets, are known for painful stings that can be inflicted over and over again. Waving your arms or striking at a wasp can provoke it, so the best defence is to remain still. • Wasp colonies live in papery nests made of wood fibre that has been chewed into a pulp. The queen lives in the nest, laying eggs, while infertile female workers care for the queen and the new larvae, and expand and defend the nest. New queens emerge in fall and mate, and then overwinter in hollow logs, under bark or under leaf litter. The founding queen and workers die and the abandoned nest decomposes overwinter. **Where found:** throughout Ontario.

Bumble Bees

Bombus **spp.**

Length: 14–20 mm

Fuzzy, docile bumble bees collect nectar and pollen, pollinating flowers in the process. • A colony's lifecycle begins in the spring, when young queens emerge from hibernation to begin feeding and constructing their underground nests. Inside each nest, a queen builds wax pots, making honey to fill some pots and rearing 8–10 grubs in others. The grubs grow into worker bees, which busy themselves all summer collecting pollen and making honey to feed the queen and the next brood of grubs. As autumn approaches, drones mate with a newly hatched queen, which then goes into hibernation while all the other bees die. **Where found:** throughout Ontario.

Harvestmen

Order Opiliones

Length: about 5 mm (body only)

These familiar, harmless bugs are usually called "daddy longlegs" but are officially known as harvestmen. • Unlike true spiders, a harvestman cannot produce silk and does not have poison glands. Its body appears oval because the head and abdomen are nearly joined. • These 8-legged arachnids use their second, longer pair of legs as antennae. They prey on smaller insects, scavenge dead animals or bugs and eat fungi and rotting plants. • Opilione fossils that date back 400 million years look much like the harvestmen we see today. **Where found:** gardens, forests, fields.

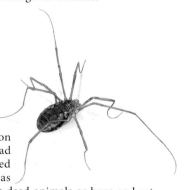

Banded Garden Spider

Argiope trifasciata

Length: *Female:* 19–28 mm; *Male:* 5–9 mm

This large, striking spider has yellow or orange markings on its shiny, black abdomen and belongs to the orb-weaver group, like the famous spider in *Charlotte's Web.* • The banded garden spider spins a web, then sedates trapped prey with a venomous bite. • A male attracts a female's attention by plucking at the edge of her web, beginning a "vibrant" relationship. Once mated, the female lays up to 3 round, papery egg sacks containing as many as 1400 eggs. The female dies soon after laying her eggs, and the hatchlings emerge in the fall. **Where found:** sunny areas near tall plants or flowers.

Dark Fishing Spider

Dolomedes tenebrosus

Length: *Female:* body 2.5 cm, legs 7.5 cm; *Male:* about 1.2 cm

What hairy beast has 8 eyeballs, dwells in dark corners, can run over water and may lurk in your basement? A fishing spider, of course. These spiders chase prey, including water striders and other insects, over the surface of the water and may even dive underneath when frightened. They are reputed to eat small fish, but whether they actually do is difficult to verify. • Dark fishing spiders are usually found near water but may wander fairly far from aquatic environments into dry forests, suburban backyards or basements. **Where found:** wetlands or lake margins; occasionally in houses.

House Centipede

Scutigera coleoptrata

Length: up to 30 mm.

Squiggly centipedes are easy to find snaking around gardens, and they sometimes crawl into houses. These rusty orange critters twist quickly over the soil, disappearing into the tiniest crevices. They prey on insects, using 2 venomous front claws to paralyze prey. Although Ontario centipedes do not generally harm people, they can inflict a painful bite when handled. • Centipedes have one pair of legs sticking out from each body segment, unlike millipedes (Order Julida) that are longer and have 2 pairs of legs underneath each body segment. **Where found:** on or under moist soil and leaf litter.

PLANTS

Plants belong to the Kingdom Plantae. They are autotrophic, which means that they produce their own food from inorganic materials through a process called photosynthesis. Plants are the basis of all food webs. They supply oxygen to the atmosphere, modify climate, and create and hold down soil. They disperse their seeds and pollen through carriers such as wind or animals. Fossil fuels come from ancient deposits of organic matter—largely that of plants. In this book, plants are separated into 3 categories: trees, shrubs, and herbs, grasses and ferns.

TREES

Trees are long-lived, woody plants that are normally taller than 5 m. There are 2 types of trees: coniferous and broadleaf. Conifers, or cone-bearers, have needles or small, scalelike leaves. Most conifers are evergreens, but larches, bald-cypress (*Taxodium distichum*) and dawn redwood (*Metasequoia glyptostroboides*) shed their leaves in winter. Most broadleaf trees lose their leaves in autumn and are often called deciduous trees (meaning "falling off" in Latin). Some exceptions include rhododendrons and several hollies.

Trees are important to various ecosystems. A single tree can provide a home or a food source for many different animals. A group of trees can provide windbreak, camouflage or shelter, hold down soil and control runoff. A forest that is large and diverse in its structure and composition (species variety, understorey, age, density) defines the community of species that live within it. The integrity of a forest relies on having a large enough area and a variety of plant species of different ages. Old-growth forest is critical habitat for many species that use the fallen or hollowed out trees as nesting or denning sites. Many species of invertebrates live within or under the bark, providing food for birds. Fallen, decomposing logs provide habitat for mosses, fungi and invertebrates. The logs eventually completely degrade into nutrient-rich soil to perpetuate the continued growth of plant life and retain organic matter in the ecosystem. Large forests retain carbon dioxide, an important preventive factor of global warming, and responsibly managed forests can sustain an industry that provides wood products and jobs.

Pine Family
pp. 142–45

White-cedar
p. 146

Elms
p. 146

Butternut & Hickory
p. 147

Beeches & Oaks
pp. 148–49

Birches
p. 150

Aspens & Poplars
pp. 151–52

**Cherries, Mountain-ash
& Hawthorns,** pp. 152–53

Sumac
p. 154

Basswood
p. 154

Dogwood
p. 155

Maples
pp. 155–57

Ashes
p. 157

Balsam Fir

Abies balsamea

Height: 10–25 m
Needles: 1.5–2.5 cm long, flat, flexible
Seed cones: 4–10 cm long, erect, dark purple when young

The barrel-shaped cones of the balsam fir usually stand straight up and grow near the top of the tree's spire-like crown. • Balsam fir is a popular choice as a Christmas tree, because cut trees do not immediately shed their needles. The wood is used mainly as pulp, and the resin, sold as "Canada balsam," is used as a mounting material for microscope slides, in glue and in candle and soap making. Traditionally, the resin was used as an antiseptic. • The bark of young trees is smooth and greyish, but mature trees have brownish, irregularly scaly bark. **Where found:** low, swampy ground to well-drained hillsides; requires moist soil; southern ¾ of Ontario. **Also known as:** Canada balsam, Canada fir, white fir.

White Spruce

Picea glauca

Height: up to 25 m
Needles: 1.5–2 cm
Seed cones: 1.5–6 cm, pale brown when mature

Look for small white spruce growing beneath old jack pines. • White spruce can live for 200 years. It is a good choice for landscaping and is often used in reforestation. • Spruce have stiff, 4-sided needles that will roll between your fingers, unlike the flat, 2-sided needles of fir. • Traditionally, Native peoples used the flexible roots to lace together birchbark canoes. • White spruce is an important source of food and shelter for many forest animals, including grouse and seed-eating birds, porcupines and red squirrels. **Where found:** various soils and climates, but prefers moist, rich soil; throughout Ontario except in the extreme south. **Also known as:** Canadian spruce, cat spruce, skunk spruce, pasture spruce.

Black Spruce

Picea mariana

Height: 5–20 m
Needles: 8–15 mm long, 4-sided, stiff
Seed cones: 2–3 cm long, dull greyish
brown to purplish brown

This slow-growing wetland tree may
live up to 200 years. • Black spruce is
an important source of lumber and
pulp. • Northern explorers used this
tree to make spruce beer, a popular
drink that prevented scurvy.
Spruce gum was also chewed or
boiled into cough syrup to
relieve sore throats, but spruce
should be used in moderation.
• Snowshoe hares love to eat young
spruce seedlings, and red squirrels
harvest the cones. **Where found:**
well-drained, moist flatlands in
the north to cool, damp sites in the south; throughout Ontario except in the
extreme south. **Also known as:** bog spruce, swamp spruce, water spruce.

Tamarack

Larix laricina

Height: up to 25 m
Needles: 2–5 cm long, soft, deciduous
Seed cones: 1–2 cm long, pale brown when mature

These slender, exotic-looking trees differ from most
conifers in that their leaves turn bright yellow and
drop in autumn. The soft needles are pale blue-
green and grow on stubby twigs, in tightly spiralled
tufts of 15–60. • Straight tamarack trunks are
often used as poles, piers and railway ties. The
tannin-rich bark was traditionally used for
tanning leather. The sap contains a natural
sugar gelatin that tastes like bitter honey.
• European larch (*L. decidua* or *L. europaea*) has
larger cones (2.5–3 cm) and is often used in
landscaping and reforestation. **Where found:**
prefers moist, well-drained soils; also in bogs and
muskeg; throughout Ontario to tundra. **Also known
as:** American larch, eastern larch, hackmatack.

Eastern Hemlock

Tsuga canadensis

Height: up to 30 m
Needles: 1–2 cm long, flat, flexible
Seed cones: 1.2–2 cm long, light brown and dry when mature

These attractive, feathery trees are popular as windbreaks and ornamentals, and lend themselves well to trimming. The needles are flat, blunt, unequal and grow in 2 opposite rows. The crushed needles were thought to smell like poison-hemlock plants, hence the common name. • These long-lived trees have a life-span of up to 600 years, with some living for a millennium. • The brittle wood separates easily along annual rings, making it easy to split, but it often "pops" and sparks when burned as firewood. • Eastern hemlock provides an abundant food supply and dense cover for many animals, including white-tailed deer, snowshoe hares, seed-eating birds, wild turkeys and grouse. **Where found:** cool, moist sites; southern ⅓ of Ontario. **Also known as:** Canada hemlock, hemlock spruce.

Eastern White Pine

Pinus strobus

Height: up to 30 m
Needles: 5–15 cm long, slender, flexible
Seed cones: 8–20 cm long, light brown and woody when mature

Eastern white pine is easily recognizable by its long, slender cones and needles in bundles of 5. This pine is often used in landscaping and reforestation. • This valuable softwood lumber is made into various products from matchsticks to doors and furniture. The Royal Navy once used the tall, straight trunks for ship masts. • The name *strobus* means a "gum-yielding" or "pitchy tree" in Latin or "cone" in Greek. **Where found:** dry, rocky ridges to sphagnum bogs; prefers humid sites with well-drained soil; southern ½ of Ontario. **Also known as:** northern white pine, Weymouth pine, soft pine.

Red Pine

Pinus resinosa

Height: up to 25 m
Needles: 10–16 cm long, brittle, in 2s
Seed cones: 4–7 cm long, light brown and woody when mature

Red pine is our only native 2-needled pine with long needles. The brittle needles snap easily (the similar Austrian pine, *P. nigra*, has flexible needles). • The colourful, reddish or pinkish bark makes red pine an attractive ornamental tree. Its deep root system and ability to grow in poor soil and open sites make it a good choice as a windbreak or for watershed protection. • The hard wood allows preservatives to penetrate, making it ideal for railway ties, bridges and structural uses. • Red squirrels and many songbirds including pine siskins, pine grosbeaks and crossbills eat the seeds of this tree. Chipmunks and other small mammals also gather seeds from the ground. **Where found:** dry, sandy or rocky areas; prefers slightly acidic, sandy soil; southern ⅔ of Ontario. **Also known as:** Norway pine.

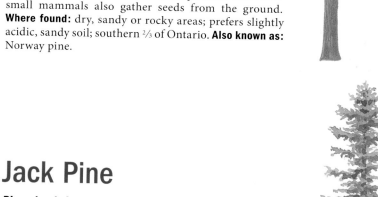

Jack Pine

Pinus banksiana

Height: up to 20 m
Needles: 2–4 cm long, straight, slightly twisted
Seed cones: 2.5–7.5 cm long, yellowish brown when mature

Jack pines are often the first conifers to colonize a burned area. The cones are held shut with a tight resin bond that melts when heated, allowing the seeds to disperse. Cones usually occur in groups of 2 or 3 and point forward on the branch. The similar Scots pine (*P. sylvestris*) has longer, twisted needles, also in groups of 2, and reddish, scaly bark. • A variety of animals and birds browse on young jack pine seedlings and eat the fallen seeds. The endangered Kirtland's warbler depends on young, pure stands for nesting. **Where found:** dry, infertile, acidic, often sandy or rocky soils; throughout Ontario except in the south and northeast. **Also known as:** Banksian pine, black pine, grey pine, scrub pine.

Eastern White-Cedar

Thuja occidentalis

Height: up to 15 m
Needles: 2–4 mm long, scale-like
Seed cones: 7–12 mm long, pale red-brown

The Niagara Escarpment is home to several ancient eastern white-cedars that are over 700 years old. One 1050-year-old cedar is the oldest tree in Canada east of British Columbia. • Also known as arborvitae, or "tree of life," eastern white-cedar was used by both Native peoples and French settlers to prevent scurvy. • Fragrant cedar lumber is known for resisting decay, but living trees are often hollow from heart-rot. The wood is commonly used in cedar-strip canoes, shingles and dock posts. **Where found:** prefers humid habitats with high snowfall and calcium-rich soils; throughout the southern ⅔ of Ontario. **Also known as:** eastern arborvitae, northern white-cedar, eastern thuja, swamp-cedar, tree-of-life.

White Elm

Ulmus americana

Height: up to 24 m
Leaves: 10–15 cm long, oval, prominently veined
Flowers: small, in tassel-like clusters
Fruit: winged nutlets, 8–10 mm long

Large, graceful elm trees once lined city streets and parks in southern Ontario, but most have now been lost to Dutch elm disease. This fungal infection was transported to Canada in the early 1940s in infected wooded crates, and it quickly wiped out hundreds of thousands of elms. The spores are carried between trees by 2 species of bark beetles. The fungus cuts off the tree's sap flow, causing it to wilt and die. Municipalities attempt to conserve their elms by monitoring, removing diseased trees and injecting fungicide into the root system, but prevention and control methods have been costly and largely ineffective. **Where found:** generally moist bottomlands and protected slopes; southern ⅔ of Ontario. **Also known as:** American elm, grey elm, soft elm, water elm.

Butternut

Juglans cinerea

Height: 12–25 m
Leaves: 30–60 cm long, divided into 11–17 leaflets
Flowers: tiny; male in hanging catkins 6–14 cm long; female in erect catkins
Fruit: green, lemon-shaped nuts, 4–6 cm long

This member of the walnut family has delicious, edible nuts, but the sticky, slightly hairy husks can be tough to shell. Nuts hang singly or in groups and contain a resin that can stain skin and clothing. In fact, a dye made from the husks and root bark was used during the American Civil War to colour soldier's uniforms. • An introduced fungus that causes the trees to develop inky black cankers is rapidly killing butternuts throughout their range. **Where found:** dry, rocky sites to moist, rich areas; usually with maples; southern ⅓ of Ontario. **Also known as:** white walnut, lemon walnut, oilnut.

Bitternut Hickory

Carya cordiformis

Height: 15–25 m
Leaves: 15–30 cm long, divided into 7–11 leaflets
Flowers: tiny; male in hanging clusters 7–10 cm long; female erect
Fruit: round nuts, 2–3.5 cm across

Bitternut hickory is Canada's most widespread hickory and our only native pecan hickory. • The wood is used for smoking ham and bacon, giving a unique hickory-smoke flavour. The strong, shock-absorbing wood is a favourite for tool handles, wooden wheels and sporting goods. Bitternut hickory can be recognized by a yellow terminal bud and the yellowish nuts, which are enclosed in a 4-ridged husk. Like their name suggests, the nuts are very bitter and inedible. The husks of all hickory nuts split into 4, a feature that distinguishes them from closely related walnuts, which have a whole or smooth fruit husk. **Where found:** sheltered, moist, rich woods from swamps to drier hillsides; southeastern Ontario. **Also known as:** swamp hickory.

American Beech

Fagus grandifolia

Height: 18–25 m
Leaves: 5–15 cm long
Flowers: tiny; male in dense, hanging clusters; female in small, erect clusters
Fruit: small, prickly burs, about 2 cm long

Beech trees produce edible nuts enclosed in a bristly, greenish to reddish brown, triangular husk. They are said to taste best after the first frost, but should be eaten in moderation to avoid an upset stomach. Traditionally, ground, roasted beech nuts were used as a coffee substitute, or the oil was extracted and used as both food and lamp oil. Beech nuts have a high fat content and are an important food source for many animals, from squirrels to black bears. • Another member of the beech family, the American chestnut (*Castanea dentata*), also has edible nuts enclosed in spiny husks and grows in our Carolinian forest. **Where found:** moist, well-drained slopes and bottomlands; southern ⅓ of Ontario. **Also known as:** red beech.

Bur Oak

Quercus macrocarpa

Height: 12–18 m
Leaves: 10–25 cm long, shiny, lobed
Flowers: tiny; male in hanging catkins; female reddish, in clusters
Fruit: acorns, 2–3 cm across

The majestic and widespread bur oak is a member of the white oak group that includes bur, white (*Q. alba*) and English (*Q. robur*) oaks. These oaks have large, rounded leaf lobes and sweet, edible acorns. The acorns can be eaten raw, but were traditionally ground or roasted and used as a flour substitute, soup thickener or caffeine-free coffee substitute. • Bur oaks are often grown in city parks and gardens as shade trees or ornamentals. Their deep roots and thick bark make them fire and drought resistant. **Where found:** deep, rich bottomlands to rocky uplands, mixed with other trees; Lake of the Woods to Thunder Bay and in the southern ⅓ of Ontario. **Also known as:** blue oak, mossy oak, mossycup oak, scrubby oak.

Red Oak

Quercus rubra

Height: 18–25 m
Leaves: 10–20 cm long, yellowish green, lobed
Flowers: tiny; male in hanging catkins
10–13 cm long; female in clusters
Fruit: acorns, 1.2–2.8 cm across

Red oak is a common eastern tree with 7–11 nearly triangular leaf lobes. • Members of the red or black oak group, which includes red, black (*Q. velutina*) and pin (*Q. palustris*) oaks, have deep, pointed leaf lobes, bitter acorns that ripen in 2 years and non-scaly bark. • The wood's varying grain and durability make red oak a favourite for hardwood flooring, furniture and dry storage barrels. Its porous grain makes the wood susceptible to rot in moist conditions. • The acorns are bitter and contain tannins toxic to humans, but they are an important food source for squirrels, raccoons, black bears, white-tailed deer and various birds. **Where found:** prefers dry, sunny slopes; southern ⅓ of Ontario. **Also known as:** eastern red oak, grey oak, northern red oak.

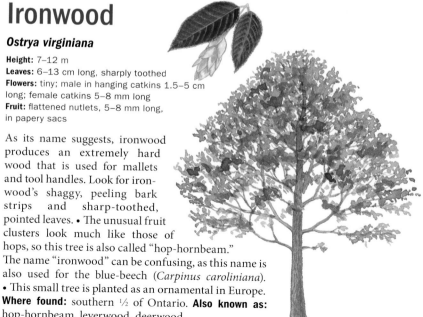

Ironwood

Ostrya virginiana

Height: 7–12 m
Leaves: 6–13 cm long, sharply toothed
Flowers: tiny; male in hanging catkins 1.5–5 cm long; female catkins 5–8 mm long
Fruit: flattened nutlets, 5–8 mm long, in papery sacs

As its name suggests, ironwood produces an extremely hard wood that is used for mallets and tool handles. Look for ironwood's shaggy, peeling bark strips and sharp-toothed, pointed leaves. • The unusual fruit clusters look much like those of hops, so this tree is also called "hop-hornbeam." The name "ironwood" can be confusing, as this name is also used for the blue-beech (*Carpinus caroliniana*). • This small tree is planted as an ornamental in Europe. **Where found:** southern ½ of Ontario. **Also known as:** hop-hornbeam, leverwood, deerwood.

Yellow Birch

Betula alleghaniensis

Height: 15–25 m
Leaves: 6–13 cm long, yellowish green, toothed
Flowers: tiny; male in hanging catkins 2–8 cm long;
female in erect catkins 1.5–2 cm long
Fruit: flat, 2-winged nutlets, in erect catkins

Birch trees are easily identified by the horizontal lenticels that mark their thin bark. Canada's birches are divided into 2 groups: yellow birches, which include yellow and cherry birch (*B. lenta*), and white birches, which include paper, Alaska (*B. neoalaskana*), water (*B. occidentalis*) and grey (*B. poulifolia*) birches. Members of the yellow birch group have oval leaves with 16–24 veins, slender, cone-like catkins and inner bark that smells like wintergreen. • Yellow birch wood is used in tool handles, hardwood floors and furniture. The sap can be boiled into syrup or fermented into beer, and the leaves and twigs can be steeped into a fragrant tea. **Where found:** rich, moist, often shady sites; southern ½ of Ontario. **Also known as:** swamp birch, curly birch, gold birch.

Paper Birch

Betula papyrifera

Height: 15–25 m
Leaves: 5–10 cm long
Flowers: tiny; male in hanging catkins 7–9 cm long; female in erect catkins 1–3 cm long
Fruit: 2-winged nutlets, in hanging catkins 3–5 cm long

Paper birch is easily recognized by its peeling, creamy white bark. This well-known tree occurs in forests across Canada and was widely used by Native peoples for birchbark canoes, baskets and message paper. To shield against snow blindness, "sunglasses" were made from bark strips with lenticels. • This pioneer species thrives in full sunlight and nutrient-rich habitats and is often the first to colonize burned or cut areas. • Birch bark is a winter staple for moose and white-tailed deer. Porcupines and snowshoe hares browse on the leaves, seedlings and bark. **Where found:** open, often disturbed sites and forest edges on a variety of substrates; throughout Ontario except on tundra and in the extreme south. **Also known as:** white birch, canoe birch, silver birch, spoolwood.

Large-toothed Aspen

Populus grandidentata

Height: 15–25 m
Leaves: 5–10 cm long, coarsely toothed
Flowers: tiny; in slender, hanging catkins 10–12 cm long
Fruit: capsules, 6–7 mm long, in hanging catkins
10–12 cm long

Large-toothed aspen, like trembling aspen, is a fast-growing, pioneer tree that sprouts up after forest fires or cutting. These sun-loving trees grow from seed or spread from suckers. Aspens reach maturity after 20 years and live only 60 years, dying off as large evergreens dominate the forest. • The buds, bark, leaves and twigs of large-toothed aspen provide food for many mammals and birds, including moose, deer, rabbits, quail and grouse. • In spring, watch for this tree's hairy, whitish buds and long, downy catkins. **Where found:** upland habitats, largest on moist, fertile sites, scrubby on dry, poor sites. **Also known as:** big-toothed aspen, big-tooth poplar, large-tooth poplar.

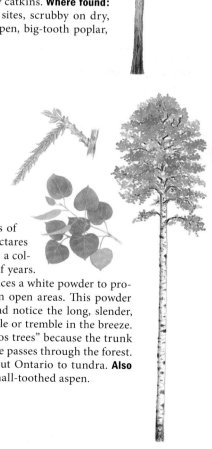

Trembling Aspen

Populus tremuloides

Height: 10–20 m
Leaves: 2–8 cm long, finely toothed
Flowers: tiny; in slender, hanging catkins
Fruit: pointed capsules, 5–7 mm long,
in hanging catkins 2–10 cm long

Suckers from the shallow, spreading roots of this deciduous tree can colonize many hectares of land. Single trunks are short-lived, but a colony of clones can survive for thousands of years. • The greenish, photosynthetic bark produces a white powder to protect the trees from ultraviolet radiation in open areas. This powder can be used as sunscreen. • Pick a leaf and notice the long, slender, flattened stem that allows the leaf to wobble or tremble in the breeze. • These trees are sometimes called "asbestos trees" because the trunk will not burn easily when a fast-moving fire passes through the forest. **Where found:** dry to moist sites; throughout Ontario to tundra. **Also known as:** quaking aspen, aspen poplar, small-toothed aspen.

Balsam Poplar

Populus balsamifera

Height: 10–25 m
Leaves: 5–12 cm long, dark green above, pale beneath
Flowers: tiny; in slender, hanging catkins
Fruit: capsules, 5–8 mm long, in hanging catkins

The trunks of these trees can reach girths of up to 1 metre, with the bark becoming deeply furrowed and dark grey when old. This tree had several traditional uses in Native medicines, as well as being a source of sugar, fragrance, ink and firewood. • The seeds are in capsules attached to parachutes of cottony down. Young seedlings have extremely large leaves to ensure maximum energy absorption. • Ungulates browse on the young trees, and bees collect the sticky, aromatic resin from the buds to cement and waterproof their hives. **Where found:** moist, low-lying areas; throughout Ontario to tundra. **Also known as:** hackmatack, tacamahac, hamatack, balsam.

Pin Cherry

Prunus pensylvanica

Height: up to 12 m
Leaves: 4–15 cm long, lance-shaped
Flowers: white, 1 cm wide, 5 petals, in clusters
Fruit: red drupes, 6–8 mm across

Pin cherries have a lifespan of about 40 years, and mature trees produce edible, sour fruit. • The stones, bark, wood and leaves of cherry trees contain hydrocyanic acid and are toxic, so only the cherry flesh can be used. • Pin cherries can also be planted as ornamentals, and flowering plants attract an audible number of bees in spring. Songbirds feast on the berries and disperse the seeds, giving rise to the name "bird cherry." • The closely related chokecherry (*P. virginiana*) has long, bottlebrush-like clusters of flowers and hanging clusters of shiny drupes. It is found on dry to moist slopes in the southern ⅔ of Ontario. **Where found:** open woodlands or recently burned sites; throughout Ontario, except on tundra. **Also known as:** bird cherry, fire cherry.

American Mountain-ash

Sorbus americana

Height: 4–10 m
Leaves: divided into 11–17 leaflets, each 5–10 cm
Flowers: tiny, white, in flat-topped clusters
Fruit: orange-red, berry-like pomes, 4–6 mm across

Deep green, glossy leaves and showy clusters of white flowers or glossy "berries" identify American mountain-ash. The juicy berries also attract many birds. They last well as decorations and are sometimes made into jams and jellies. • Two other mountain-ash species occur in Ontario: the similar, native, showy mountain-ash (*S. decora*) has slightly narrower leaflets; the introduced eastern mountain-ash (*S. aucuparia*) has downy buds and hairier leaves. **Where found:** moist, shady sites; south-eastern ½ of Ontario. **Also known as:** American rowan-tree, dogberry, rowanberry.

Hawthorns

Crataegus spp.

Height: up to 6 m
Leaves: 2–9 cm long
Flowers: usually white to pinkish, 1–1.5 cm across, in flat-topped clusters
Fruit: red haws (pomes), 8–10 mm across

Several hawthorn species grow in Ontario, and these trees or tall shrubs are often planted as ornamentals. Most have branched clusters of white, unpleasant-smelling flowers and reddish haws that remain on the plant throughout winter. To identify hawthorns, look for the thorny branches and larger leaves growing off the flowering shoots. • Leaves, flowers and extracts of hawthorn may be used to treat a range of ailments, from coughs to back pain. **Where found:** open or gravelly sites near water; southern ½ of Ontario.

Staghorn Sumac

Rhus typhina

Height: up to 6 m
Leaves: 30–50 cm long,
divided into 11–31 leaflets,
each 8–13 cm long
Flowers: tiny, greenish, in
erect clusters
Fruit: red, fuzzy drupes, 3–5 mm
across, in erect, cone-like clusters

Staghorn sumac is sometimes planted as an ornamental for its showy, red fruit clusters and colourful autumn leaves. In winter, the wide, woolly branches resemble velvet-covered deer antlers, inspiring the name "staghorn." • A black ink was made from boiling the fruit and leaves, and dried autumn leaves were sometimes rolled and smoked. The ripe fruit can be eaten raw or made into jelly. Delicious, pink lemonade can be made by soaking crushed fruit in cold water (to remove the hairs), then sweetening with sugar. **Where found:** open, often disturbed sites, typically on dry, rocky or sandy soil; southern ½ of Ontario. **Also known as:** velvet sumac, sumac vinegar-tree.

American Basswood

Tilia americana

Height: 18–22 m
Leaves: 12–15 cm long, sharply toothed
Flowers: yellowish, 1.1–1.3 cm across, in
loose, hanging clusters
Fruit: woolly, nut-like capsules, 6–8 mm
across

Basswoods, with their fragrant flowers, large leaves and rounded crowns, are often planted in urban parks and gardens. Stump sprouts lend themselves well to transplanting. • The soft wood is ideal for carving and is also used for furniture, measuring sticks and pulp. The tough inner bark fibres were once woven into ropes, nets and clothing. Linden flower tea provides a remedy for coughs, colds and bronchitis. • Bees are attracted to the hanging flower clusters. **Where found:** cool, moist, rich woods, often near water and mixed with other hardwoods; southern ½ of Ontario. **Also known as:** American linden, whitewood, bee-tree, lime-tree.

Eastern Flowering Dogwood

Cornus florida

Height: 3–10 m
Leaves: 5–15 cm long, wavy-edged
Flowers: tiny, greenish, surrounded
by 4 petal-like bracts
Fruit: berry-like drupes, 1–1.5 cm long

This beautiful, small understorey
tree has delicate flowers, shiny
red berries and red autumn
leaves. The showy, whitish
dogwood "flowers" are actually floral
bracts that surround the true clusters of tiny,
greenish flowers. • Golf-club heads, daggers and
engraver's blocks have been made from the tough
wood. • The berries attract birds and provide food
for small mammals. • Unfortunatley, many
eastern flowering dogwoods have been lost to
wood anthracnose, a fungal disease. **Where found:**
in and around wet or sandy woodlands and ravines; southeastern Ontario.
Also known as: arrow-wood, bitter red-cherry, common dogwood, dogtree.

Sugar Maple

Acer saccharum

Height: 20–35 m
Leaves: 8–20 cm long, 5-lobed, irregularly toothed
Flowers: tiny, yellow-green, in clusters
Fruit: winged samaras, 2–4 cm long, in pairs

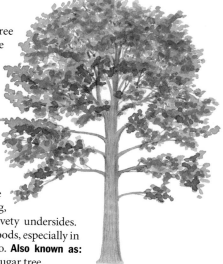

The sugar maple is Canada's national tree
and the source of the stylized red maple
leaf on our flag. • Sugar maples are
famous worldwide for their sap, the
main source of pure maple syrup and
tasty maple sugar. Each spring, "sugar-
ing off" festivals are held across Ontario
to celebrate the tradition of boiling sap
and making maple syrup. About 40 litres
of sap yields 1 litre of maple syrup.
• Look for the maple's winged seeds, which
helicopter downward when shed. • Sugar
maple often hybridizes with black maple
(*A. nigrum*). Black maple has drooping,
blunt-pointed, deep green leaves with velvety undersides.
Where found: deep, rich soils in fairly dry woods, especially in
calcareous regions; southern ½ of Ontario. **Also known as:**
rock maple, hard maple, bird's-eye maple, sugar tree.

Silver Maple

Acer saccharinum

Height: 20–30 m
Leaves: 8–15 cm long, 5–7-lobed, irregularly toothed
Flowers: tiny, yellow or reddish, in clusters
Fruit: winged samaras, 4–7 cm long, in pairs

Fast-growing, hardy silver maples are often planted as ornamentals, but their heavy leaf and seed fall, brittle branches and aggressive root system may prove to be troublesome. This tree gets its name from the silvery-white undersides of the leaves. • Silver maple wood lacks strength and is mainly for crates, veneer or pulp. A delicately flavoured syrup can be made from boiling the sap, though it is not as sweet as sugar maple sap. • The often hollow trunks of silver maple provide nesting cavities for wood ducks and other birds, dens for mammals and hiding places for small children. **Where found:** moist to wet sites near streams, swamps and lakes; southern ½ of Ontario. **Also known as:** soft maple, white maple, river maple.

Red Maple

Acer rubrum

Height: 20–25 m
Leaves: 5–15 cm long, 3–5-lobed, irregularly toothed
Flowers: tiny, reddish, 3 mm wide, in clusters
Fruit: winged samaras, 1.5–2.5 cm long, in pairs

The red twigs, buds, flowers and autumn leaves of this common maple add colour to North America's eastern forests. The bright red, tassel-like flower clusters appear early in spring. • Red maple leaves have 3–5 palmate lobes, which are separated by shallow notches. The samara wings spread at a 60° angle. • The even, straight-grained wood is used in cabinets, furniture and flooring, and the bark can be boiled into a red ink or dark brown dye. The sap yields a syrup that is not too sweet. **Where found:** cool, moist sites near swamps, streams and springs; sometimes in drier upland sites; southern ⅓ of Ontario. **Also known as:** scarlet maple, soft maple, swamp maple, curled maple.

Mountain Maple

Acer spicatum

Height: 3–5 m
Leaves: 5–12 cm long, 3-lobed, toothed
Flowers: 6 mm across, yellowish green, in erect clusters
Fruit: winged samaras, 1.8–2 cm long, in pairs

This small maple is our most northerly ranging species, found well into the boreal forest. It is identified in summer by opposite leaves with 3 prominent lobes and small scarlet to pinkish brown samaras. • Mountain maple has no commercial value, but the branches spread toward the ground, take root and grow into dense thickets, controlling erosion on steep banks and ravines. **Where found:** moist, mixed woods, thickets; southern ⅔ of Ontario. **Also known as:** dwarf maple, moose maple.

Striped Maple

Acer pensylvanicum

Height: 4–10 m
Leaves: 10–18 cm long, 3-lobed, finely toothed
Flowers: 6 mm wide, greenish yellow, in drooping clusters
Fruit: winged samaras, 2.5–3 cm long, in pairs

Striped maple's long, palmate leaves are the largest of any Ontario maple. This shade-tolerant tree has long clusters of bell-shaped flowers in spring, and attractive, vertically striped bark. • Manitoba maple (*A. negundo*) is often planted as a shade tree and can grow to 20 m tall. **Where found:** cool, moist, shady woodlands; southern ⅓ of Ontario; absent in the extreme southeast. **Also known as:** moosewood, moose maple.

White Ash

Fraxinus nigra

Height: 10–20 m
Leaves: 22–45 cm long, divided into 7–11 leaflets, each 7–14 cm long
Flowers: tiny, purple, in compact clusters
Fruit: winged samaras, 2.5–4 cm long

White ash is Ontario's most common ash and the main source of commercial ash. The strong, flexible wood is often used in sporting goods, tool handles, boats and church pews. Historically, wooden plows, airplane and automobile frames were made from ash. • The crushed leaves can be used to soothe insect bites. • Black ash (*F. nigra*) is our widest-ranging ash and occurs north into swampy boreal forest woodlands. **Where found:** upland sites with rocky to deep, well-drained soils; southern ⅓ of Ontario. **Also known as:** American ash, Canadian white ash.

SHRUBS

Shrubs survive several seasons and are therefore perennials. They have one or more woody stems or can be a vine, and they are normally less than 5 m tall. Shrubs may produce flowers and fruit. They provide habitat and shelter for a variety of animals, and their berries, leaves and often bark are crucial sources of food. The tasty berries of some shrubs have been a staple of native and traditional foods, and they are still enjoyed by people throughout Ontario.

Evergreens
pp. 160–61

Alders & Birches
p. 161

Hazelnut
p. 162

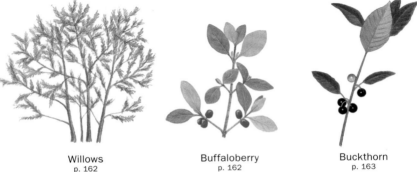

Willows
p. 162

Buffaloberry
p. 162

Buckthorn
p. 163

Dogwood
p. 163

Rose Family
pp. 164–65

Currants
pp. 165–66

Heaths
pp. 166–68

Prince's-pine
p. 169

Honeysuckle Family
pp. 169–70

Poison Ivy
p. 171

Canada Yew

Taxus canadensis

Height: up to 2 m
Needles: 1–2.5 cm long, flat
Cones: 2–3 mm long, inconspicuous
Fruit: berry-like, 7.5 mm across, single seed in a fleshy cup

Dark green, evergreen needles and bright scarlet berries make this an attractive ornamental shrub, but all parts of this plant are poisonous. • The foliage, bark and roots contain paclitaxel, which is used to treat ovarian and breast cancers. • The flowers are borne in tiny cones. • Moose and white-tailed deer seek out the twigs for winter food. **Where found:** moist, shady sites; southern ⅔ of Ontario. **Also known as:** ground hemlock.

Crowberry

Empetrum nigrum

Height: 15 cm
Leaves: 3–8 mm long, needle-like
Flowers: purplish crimson, tiny
Fruit: berry-like drupes, 4–8 mm across

This creeping, evergreen shrub forms dense mats on the forest floor. It is commonly found in muskeg, cool spruce forests and on tundra. • The dark purple, edible berries may be harvested in fall or the following spring. Native peoples ate the berries fresh or mixed them with grease. The berries can also be made into jams and jellies or added to baked goods. Bears eat large amounts of crowberries. **Where found:** coniferous forest floor, acidic peatlands and rocky slopes; throughout Ontario. **Also known as:** curlewberry.

Common Juniper

Juniperus communis

Height: 30–100 cm
Needles: 0.5–1.2 cm long, stiff
Seed cones: 0.8–1.2 cm across, fleshy, berry-like

The blue-grey "berries" of this shrub are, in fact, tiny cones with 3–8 fleshy scales. They can add spice to food and flavouring to gin, but pregnant women and people with kidney problems should never ingest them. Europeans made juniper berry tea to treat eating disorders, diarrhea and heart, lung and kidney problems. • Native peoples burned juniper branches to purify homes, ward off evil and bring good luck to hunters. • This pungent, prickly, clumped or matted evergreen produces pollen (male) and seed (female) cones on separate shrubs. **Where found:** dry, open sites; throughout Ontario.

Sand Heather

Hudsonia tomentosa

Height: 22 cm
Leaves: 2–4 mm long, scale-like, hairy
Flowers: 6 mm across, bright yellow
Fruit: smooth, oval capsules

Sand heather is a low, evergreen shrub with overlapping, scale-like leaves that resemble those of some junipers. A long root anchors this plant to shifting sand dunes and allows it to live in dry, sandy sites. Abundant, bright yellow flowers appear in late June and July. • The genus name honours English botanist William Hudson, and the species name *tomentosa* refers to the small, woolly hairs that cover the stems and leaves. **Where found:** sand hills, pine barrens; southern ⅔ of Ontario. **Also known as:** woolly hudsonia, false heather.

Green Alder

Alnus viridis

Height: 1–4 m
Leaves: 4–8 cm long, shiny, finely toothed
Flowers: in catkins; female cone-like, 1–1.5 cm long; male hanging, 3–8 cm long
Fruit: flat, 2-winged nutlets (samaras)

These tall, clumped deciduous shrubs often grow in forest understoreys. The fruits are tiny, broadly winged nutlets, shed from woody, egg-shaped clusters (female catkins). • The wood was an important fuel for smoking fish, meat and hides. The twigs and inner bark produce a red-brown dye that was used to colour hides and birchbark baskets. • Speckled alder (*A. incana*) grows near lakes and rivers and can be distinguished by its dull green, double-toothed leaves. **Where found:** streamsides and moist woods or dry uplands; throughout Ontario except in the extreme southeast. **Also known as:** *A. crispa*.

Dwarf Birch

Betula pumila

Height: up to 2 m
Leaves: 1–4 cm long, toothed
Flowers: catkins; male hanging, 12–20 mm long; female erect, 12–25 mm long
Fruit: small, winged nutlets

Dwarf birch is a common shrub of the boreal forest. The branches, with their small, attractive leaves, make a unique addition to flower arrangements. • Some Native peoples chewed the stems, then used them to make a poultice that was packed into deep cuts to stop bleeding. A tea made from the leaves and branches was said to aid in weight loss, and tea made from the cones was used to relieve menstrual cramps. **Where found:** marshes, sloughs, bogs; throughout Ontario. **Also known as:** bog birch.

Beaked Hazelnut

Corylus cornuta

Height: up to 3–4 m
Leaves: 5–12 cm long, finely double-toothed
Flowers: tiny; male in catkins up to 5 cm long;
female in clusters 3 mm long
Fruit: nuts, 3–4 cm across

Plentiful, edible wild hazelnuts are rich in protein, but sometimes become infested with grubs just when they are ready to harvest. A bristly, greenish, beaked husk surrounds each round nut. Nuts may be single or in groups of 2–3. • Native peoples used hazelnut wood for drumsticks. • If you have sharp eyes, you may spot the hazelnut's tiny, crimson red female flowers in late April or May. **Where found:** southern ¾ of Ontario. **Also known as:** beaked filbert.

Willows

Salix spp.

Height: varies, shrubs or trees up to 20 m
Leaves: varies, 2–15 cm long
Flowers: tiny, in catkins
Fruit: hairy capsules

Many willow species are found in Ontario, both shrubs and trees, and most have narrow or oblong leaves. Willows grow quickly and have extensive root systems, making them a good choice for erosion control or for revegetating burned areas. • The stems of some species are used for wickerwork or, traditionally, for dreamcatcher charms. Traditionally, wet inner bark fibres were twisted with spruce gum into fishing nets and ropes. The hollow stems were used as drinking straws or for making pipes. Green branches can be used to smoke meat. **Where found:** moist to wet sites; forests and limestone flats; throughout Ontario.

Buffaloberry

Shepherdia canadensis

Height: 1–2 m
Leaves: 1.5–6 cm long, smooth-edged
Flowers: greenish yellow, 4 mm across
Fruit: cherry-like drupes, 4–6 mm long

This deciduous shrub has dark green, silvery leaves with star-shaped hairs and rust-coloured scales. The inconspicuous, yellowish to greenish flowers are either male or female and grow on separate plants. The tempting, juicy, translucent red berries are quite sour, but many Native peoples enjoyed them. • Buffaloberries contain a bitter, soapy substance (saponin) that foams when beaten. They were traditionally whipped like egg whites to make a foamy dessert, which was sweetened with other berries, and later with sugar. **Where found:** open woods and streambanks; throughout Ontario. **Also known as:** soapberry, rabbitberry.

Alder-leaved Buckthorn

Rhamnus alnifolia

Height: <1 m
Leaves: 4–10 cm long, finely toothed
Flowers: yellowish green, 3 mm long
Fruit: berry-like drupes, 6–8 mm across

Alder-leaved buckthorn has tapered leaves with 6–8 prominent, nearly straight veins and small flowers that grow in clusters.
• **Caution:** All parts of this plant, including the berries, contain glycosides that can cause vomiting and diarrhea. Racoons, grey catbirds and
brown thrashers are able to eat the fruit. • Common or European buckthorn (*R. cathartica*) is an introduced species that grows up to 6 m tall along
roadsides and in moist woodlands or fields of southern Ontario. **Where found:**
moist, shady woods; throughout Ontario to tundra.

Red-osier Dogwood

Cornus sericea

Height: 0.5–3 m
Leaves: 2–10 cm
Flowers: <5 mm across, white, in flat-topped clusters
Fruit: berry-like drupes, about 5–7 mm across

This attractive, hardy, deciduous shrub has distinctive
purple to red branches with white flowers in spring,
red leaves in autumn, and white "berries" in winter. It is
easily grown from cuttings. • Native peoples smoked the dried inner bark
alone or with tobacco or common bearberry (kinnikinnick). The flexible
branches were often woven into baskets by Native peoples, but also provide food
for squirrels and birds. • Alternate-leaf dogwood (*C. alternifolia*) grows to 6 m tall
and has alternate leaves, unlike typical, opposite-leaved dogwoods. **Where found:**
moist sites; throughout Ontario. **Also known as:** *C. stolonifera*.

Narrow-leaved Meadowsweet

Spiraea alba **var.** *latifolia*

Height: up to 1.5 m
Leaves: 3–6 cm long, finely toothed
Flowers: white, 5–8 mm across, in dense clusters
Fruit: clusters of small pods

Narrow-leaved meadowsweet's tall, pyramid-shaped flower clusters
appear throughout summer. The flower clusters look slightly fuzzy
because they are covered in fine hairs. Mature branches have purplish
grey, peeling bark. • The leaves of this plant were traditionally steeped
into a flavourful tea. **Where found:** moist sandy or rocky sites, riparian
areas, lakeshores, ditches. **Also known as:** white meadowsweet.

Red-twigged Serviceberry

Amelanchier sanguinea

Height: 1–3 m
Leaves: 3–7 cm long, finely toothed
Flowers: white, 4–8 mm across, 5 narrow petals
Fruit: dark purple, berry-like pomes, 5–10 mm wide

These hardy, deciduous shrubs or small trees have beautiful blossoms in spring, delicious fruit in summer and scarlet leaves in autumn. • The sweet, juicy "berries" were an important food source for many Native peoples. Today, serviceberries are used in baked goods, jams, jellies, syrups and wine. Many mammals and birds also feast on them. • Mountain juneberry (*A. bartramiana*) is shorter, has small clusters of 1–4 flowers and fine, sharply toothed leaves. It grows north to the tundra. **Where found:** dry, often sandy woods, rocky sites; southern ⅔ of Ontario. **Also known as:** roundleaf juneberry, roundleaf serviceberry.

Cloudberry

Rubus chamaemorus

Height: 5–20 cm
Leaves: 2–7 cm across, 5–7 lobes, toothed
Flowers: white, 2 cm across
Fruit: raspberry-like drupelets, in 1.5 cm clusters

There is something magical about cloudberries. Perhaps it's that the luscious berries seem to float above the stems or that something so juicy can be borne out of the tundra. These "berries" were an important fruit for northern Native peoples, second only to blueberries. • Fresh cloudberries should be eaten right away, before they become mushy. They make delicious jams, jellies and wine. **Where found:** boreal wetlands, sphagnum bogs, moist tundra; throughout Ontario except in the extreme southeast. **Also known as:** bakeapple.

Wild Red Raspberry

Rubus idaeus

Height: 1–2 m
Leaves: compound, 13–20 cm long, 5–7 leaflets
Flowers: white, 8–12 mm across, in clusters
Fruit: raspberries, 1 cm across

Delicious, plump raspberries are a favourite among berry pickers. The tasty fruit can be eaten straight off the bush or made into jams, jellies or pies. Fresh or completely dried leaves make excellent tea, but wilted leaves can be toxic. • Dwarf raspberry (*R. pubescens*) hugs the ground in wet areas across the boreal forest, bearing solitary red raspberries (technically a cluster of 20–30 druplets). **Where found:** thickets, clearings, open woods; throughout Ontario.

Prickly Wild Rose

Rosa acicularis

Height: 20–120 cm
Leaves: compound, 5–7 leaflets, each 2–5 cm long
Flowers: solitary, 5–7 cm across, pink
Fruit: red hips, 2–3 cm long

Because of their dense prickles and slender thorns, these sweet-smelling deciduous shrubs, with their fragrant pink roses and scarlet, berry-like hips are usually considered a nuisance. • Smooth wild rose (*R. blanda*) has slightly smaller, 1–1.5 cm long hips and only a few scattered thorns. • Most parts of rose shrubs are edible, but the sweet, nutritious hips are most commonly eaten or used to make tea. Avoid the seeds; their sliver-like hairs can irritate the digestive tract and cause "itchy bum." **Where found:** dry to moist sites; throughout Ontario.

Three-toothed Cinquefoil

Sibbaldiopsis tridentata

Height: 10–20 cm
Leaves: divided into 3 leaflets, each 1–2.5 cm long
Flowers: white, 8–10 mm across, 5 petals
Fruit: small, brown, hairy achenes

This hardy shrub is found in dry, rocky exposed areas. It has bright white blooms that appear in June and July. • The oblong leaflets are arranged in groups of 3, and each leaflet has 3 teeth at the tip. • Three-toothed cinquefoil was historically used in mouthwashes and lotion, and medicinally to relieve sore throats and fever. **Where found:** wet to dry, often rocky sites; throughout Ontario. **Also known as:** *Potentilla tridentata*.

Bristly Black Currant

Ribes lacustre

Height: 50–150 cm
Leaves: 3–4 cm wide, 5–7 deeply cut lobes
Flowers: reddish, 6 mm across, in clusters
Fruit: black berries, 5–8 mm across, bristly

The branch spines of this deciduous shrub can cause serious allergic reactions in sensitive people, and some consider the branches (and by extension, the bristly, glandular fruit) to be poisonous. • The small flowers are reddish to maroon and hang in clusters of 7–15. • Many Native groups ate the edible but insipid berries, fresh or cooked. Today, bristly black currants are usually made into jam. • Wild currants are the intermediate host for blister rust, a virulent disease of native 5-needled pines. **Where found:** moist, wooded, or open sites; throughout Ontario. **Also known as:** swamp black currant.

Skunk Currant

Ribes glandulosum

Height: up to 1 m
Leaves: 3–5.5 cm long, 5–7 lobes
Flowers: whitish to pink, 6 mm across, in clusters of 6–15
Fruit: red berries, 6 mm across, bristly

The crushed leaves and stems of this plant emit a distinct, skunk-like odour. • The bristly red berries are not very palatable, but are eaten by moose, chipmunks, martens and birds, including thrushes, thrashers and waxwings. • The roots of this plant were used medicinally to relieve back pain. • Several other *Ribes* species (currants and gooseberries) are found in various habitats throughout Ontario. All have maple-leaf-shaped leaves and red or black berries. **Where found:** damp forests, swampy areas and clearings; throughout Ontario, except on tundra.

Lingonberry

Vaccinium vitis-idaea

Height: 10–20 cm
Leaves: 6–15 mm long, leathery
Flowers: pinkish cups, 6–15 mm long
Fruit: red berries, 5–10 mm across

In northern Ontario, mixed patches of lingonberry, lichen and Labrador tea carpet the tundra in a mosaic of reddish brown. The smooth, dark green leaves have dark spots on their undersides. • The lingonberry was the third most important fruit to northern Native peoples, after blueberry and cloudberry. The acidic berries were usually collected after the first frost, and commonly used in pemmican or cooked with grease, fish or meat. Berries were boiled to make a dye for porcupine quills or were made into necklaces. **Where found:** throughout Ontario. **Also known as:** bog cranberry.

Velvet Leaf Blueberry

Vaccinium myrtilloides

Height: 10–50 cm
Leaves: 1–4 cm long, smooth-edged
Flowers: greenish white, 3–5 mm across, in clusters
Fruit: blue berries, 4–8 mm across

Plentiful blueberries were the most important fruits for northern Native peoples, and blueberry picking remains a favourite family tradition today. Traditionally the berries were eaten fresh, dried or preserved in grease. The roots and stems were boiled into various medicinal teas, used for headaches, to regulate menstruation or even prevent pregnancy (stems). Today, young and old alike enjoy blueberry pie, jam, pancakes and even blueberry wine. • Low sweet blueberry (*V. angustifolium*) occurs in similar habitats. **Where found:** sandy soils in forests and clearings; throughout Ontario. **Also known as:** common blueberry.

Dwarf Blueberry

Vaccinium caespitosum

Height: 5–30 cm
Leaves: 1–3 cm long, finely toothed
Flowers: whitish to pink, 4–5 mm across, solitary
Fruit: blue berries, 6 mm across

Dwarf blueberry has lance-shaped, toothed leaves
and is found in much of northern Ontario and Québec.
The similar, circumpolar bog bilberry (*V. uliginosum*) has ellip-
tical, smooth-edged leaves and flowers with 4 instead of 5 lobes.
Both have edible berries that were an important source of nutrition
for Native peoples. Many wild animals and birds also feed on the berries, including
black bears, foxes, small mammals, grouse and songbirds. **Where found:** northern
²/₃ of Ontario, except on tundra. **Also known as:** dwarf bilberry.

Bearberry

Arctostaphylos uva-ursi

Height: 5–15 cm
Leaves: 1–3 cm long, leathery
Flowers: 4–6 mm long, pinkish white, urn-shaped
Fruit: berry-like drupes, 0.6–1 cm across, bright red

Thick, leathery evergreen leaves help this common, mat-
forming shrub to survive on dry, sunny slopes where others
would perish. Trailing, 50- to 100-cm-long branches send
down roots, and the flowers nod in small clusters. • The red "berries" are edible,
but rather mealy and tasteless. They were traditionally cooked and mixed with
grease or fish eggs to reduce their dryness. • The glossy leaves were widely used
for smoking, both alone and later with tobacco. **Where found:** well-drained, open
or wooded sites; throughout Ontario. **Also known as:** kinnikinnick.

Trailing Arbutus

Epigaea repens

Height: trailing shrub
Leaves: 2.5–7.5 cm long
Flowers: white to pink, 1–2 cm across
Fruit: tiny capsules

The creeping stems of this evergreen shrub thrive in sandy, shady
places on the forest floor. • The tiny, funnel-shaped flowers are
edible and make an interesting addition to salads. Historically,
the leaves were used to relieve urinary tract illnesses. • Grouse
and heath voles eat the buds, leaves and seeds. • This plant is often grown as an
ornamental and grows best in sheltered, shaded areas, in soil rich in compost or
decayed leaves. **Where found:** shady sites in acidic soils or rocky woods; southeastern
²/₃ of Ontario. **Also known as:** mayflower, ground laurel.

Leatherleaf

Chamaedaphne calyculata

Height: up to 1 m
Leaves: 1–4.5 cm
Flowers: white, 5–6 mm long
Fruit: brownish capsules, up to 6 mm wide

Leatherleaf is a genuine bog species that can be found in almost every boreal bog. Patches of this low evergreen shrub can form dense thickets or floating mats at the edges of lakes or swamps. Its delicate, urn-shaped flowers grow in long clusters, then give way to fruit capsules that contain abundant tiny seeds. **Where found:** wet coniferous bogs and swamps, lakeshores; throughout Ontario. **Also known as:** cassandra.

Bog Rosemary

Andromeda glaucophylla

Height: 30–60 cm
Leaves: 2–5.5 cm long, leathery
Flowers: white to pinkish, 6 mm across
Fruit: small capsules, 6 mm across

Despite resembling and sharing the name of a common kitchen herb, bog rosemary contains poisonous andromedotoxin compounds that can cause breathing problems, vomiting and even death if ingested. • The leathery leaves of this plant curl under, and their undersides are covered with fine hairs to help prevent moisture loss. • Bog rosemary has rounded stems and bluish green, alternate leaves, unlike bog laurel (*Kalmia polifolia*), which has flattened stems and shiny, green, opposite leaves and is found in bogs and acidic lakeshores throughout Ontario, except in the southeast. **Where found:** wet areas, coniferous swamps, sphagnum bogs, lakeshores; southern ⅔ of Ontario. **Also known as:** downy rosemary.

Labrador Tea

Ledum groenlandicum

Height: 30–80 cm
Leaves: 1–5 cm long, leathery
Flowers: white, 5–8 mm across, in clusters
Fruit: drooping capsules, 5–7 mm long

This evergreen shrub saves energy by keeping its leaves year round. The leaves have a thick, leathery texture, rolled edges and distinctive reddish, woolly hairs on their undersides, all adaptations that help the plant conserve moisture. Labrador tea may also produce chemicals that discourage other plants from growing nearby. • Native peoples and early settlers made the leaves and flowers into a tea that was rich in vitamin C. **Caution:** Consuming large amounts can be toxic; do not confuse this plant with other poisonous heaths such as bog laurel or bog rosemary. **Where found:** moist, acidic, nutrient-poor soils; often associated with black spruce; throughout Ontario. **Also known as:** bog tea, woolly tea.

Prince's-pine

Chimaphila umbellata

Height: 10–30 cm
Leaves: 2–8 cm long, leathery
Flowers: white to pinkish, bell-shaped, <1 cm across
Fruit: rounded capsules, 5–7 mm across

The leaves of this semi-woody, evergreen shrub are dark, glossy green above and pale beneath. The waxy flowers grow in small clusters. These attractive plants need certain soil fungi to live, so they often die when transplanted. They are best enjoyed in the wild. • Prince's-pine has been used to flavour candy, soft drinks (especially root beer) and traditional beers. Native peoples made a tea from this plant that was used as a remedy for fluid retention, kidney or bladder problems, fevers and coughs. Several Native groups smoked the dried leaves. **Where found:** wooded, usually coniferous sites; southern ¾ of Ontario. **Also known as:** pipsissewa.

Twinflower

Linnea borealis

Height: 3–10 cm
Leaves: 1–2 cm long, rounded
Flowers: pink, bell-shaped, 6–15 mm long
Fruit: nutlets, <1.5–3 mm long

This trailing, semi-woody evergreen makes an excellent native ground cover in partially shaded sites. The small, delicate pairs of pink bells are easily overlooked among other plants on the forest floor, but their strong, sweet perfume may draw you to them in the evening. Hooked bristles on the tiny, egg-shaped nutlets catch on fur, feathers or the clothing of passersby, who then carry these inconspicuous hitchhikers to new locations. **Where found:** moist, open or shaded sites; throughout Ontario.

Bracted Honeysuckle

Lonicera involucrata

Height: 1–2 m
Leaves: 5–10 cm long, hairy
Flowers: yellow, tubular, 1–2 cm across
Fruit: shiny, black berries, <8 mm across

The unusual, shiny berries of these deciduous shrubs, with their broad, spreading, backward-bending, shiny red to purplish bracts, catch the eyes of passersby and also of hungry bears and birds. Despite their tempting appearance, these berries are unpalatable, and they can be toxic. **Where found:** moist to wet, usually shaded sites; throughout Ontario to tundra. **Also known as:** involucred fly honeysuckle, black twinberry.

Common Snowberry

Symphoricarpos albus

Height: 50–75 cm
Leaves: 2–4 cm long
Flowers: pink to white, bell-shaped, 4–7 mm long
Fruit: white drupe, 0.6–1 cm across

The name "snowberry" refers to the waxy, white "berries" that remain in small clusters near branch tips through winter. All parts of this deciduous shrub are toxic and will cause vomiting and diarrhea. • Some Native groups called the fruits "corpse berries," because they were believed to be the ghosts of saskatoons—part of the spirit world, not to be eaten by the living. • The closely related western snowberry (*S. occidentalis*) has thicker, oblong leaves and clusters of greenish white berries. **Where found:** well-drained sites; southern ⅔ of Ontario. **Also known as:** waxberry.

Nannyberry

Viburnum lentago

Height: 4–7 m
Leaves: 5–10 cm long, toothed
Flowers: white, 4–8 mm across, in clusters
Fruit: berry-like drupes, 8–12 mm

Nannyberry can be recognized by its fragrant flowers, showy, bluish black fruit and reddish winter twigs. • The edible "berries" taste like raisins and can be eaten raw or used in jams and jellies. Many wild birds, including wild turkeys, grouse and songbirds, feed on the fruit, and then disperse the seeds. **Where found:** wet, rich sites near water, roadsides and thickets; southern ⅓ of Ontario. **Also known as:** wild raisin, blackhaw.

Highbush Cranberry

Viburnum trilobum

Height: up to 4 m
Leaves: 5–11 cm long, maple-leaf-like, 3-lobed
Flowers: white, 1.5–2.5 cm wide
Fruit: berry-like drupes, 1 cm across

Shiny, red to orange highbush cranberry fruit makes a tart, tasty trailside snack, and it is easy to pick for use in jams and jellies. The berry-like fruits remain above the snow in winter. • The introduced European highbush cranberry (*V. opulus* var. *opulus*) sometimes escapes cultivation. It has bristle-like leaf stipules, and some cultivars have very showy balls of flowers. • Other viburnums with 3-lobed leaves, mapleleaf viburnum (*V. acerifolium*) and squashberry (*V. edule*), are both less than 2 m tall. **Where found:** moist, rich sites near water in cool woodlands; southern ⅔ of Ontario. **Also known as:** American cranberry bush; *V. opulus* ssp. *trilobum*.

Common Elderberry

Sambucus nigra ssp. *canadensis*

Height: 1–3 m
Leaves: compound, divided into 5–11 leaflets, each 5–15 cm long
Flowers: white, 3–6 mm across, in flat-topped clusters
Fruit: purplish black, berry-like drupes, 5–6 mm across

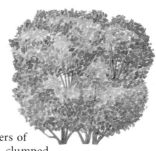

Large, showy clusters of flowers or heavy, wide clusters of "berries" draw attention to this strong-smelling, clumped, deciduous shrub. The berries can be made into jam, jelly, pies and wine, but they are unpalatable and even toxic when raw or immature. The rest of the plant is poisonous to humans, though moose, deer and elk seem to enjoy it. **Where found:** moist sites; southern ⅓ of Ontario. **Also known as:** common elder, Canada elderberry, *Sambucus canadensis*.

Poison Ivy

Toxicodendron radicans

Height: <1 m
Leaves: compound, 3 leaflets, each 5–15 cm
Flowers: greenish white, 2–3 mm across
Fruit: white berry, 5–6 mm across

Even the youngest children visiting Ontario's forests learn to recognize poison ivy's 3 leaflets. A brush with this plant causes a severe allergic reaction, obvious in an itchy rash and swelling. The rash can be alleviated by washing with plenty of soap, but if symptoms worsen, seek medical attention. Eating any part of this plant can be fatal. • Native peoples burned poison ivy leaves as enemies advanced, because the ashes carry tiny droplets of toxin through the air. **Where found:** various dry to moist upland sites; southern ⅓ of Ontario.

Riverbank Grape

Vitis riparia

Height: to 20 m or higher; climbing vine
Leaves: 7–15 cm long; 3-lobed (some unlobed), coarsely toothed
Flowers: tiny; greenish, in compact pyramidal clusters
Fruits: spherical, waxy, black with bluish caste

Riverside grape is a key parent species in breeding modern grape varieties that are disease- and cold-resistant. The small, tart fruit is juicy and flavourful, especially after the first frost. Eat them raw, made into jelly or fermented into a musky-flavoured wine. • Add a grape leaf to homemade pickle jars to keep the pickles from going soft—leaves contain a natural inhibitor that reduces the effects of a softening enzyme present on mouldy cucumber blossoms. **Where found:** moist thickets and woods; southern ON.

HERBS, GRASSES & FERNS

The plants in this section are all non-woody plants and include herbs, grasses and ferns. Herbs, grasses and ferns can be annual, though many are perennial, growing from a persistent rootstock. Most of those with flowering stems later produce fruit. Various forms of seeds are familiar, such as those of the sunflower, a favoured treat, and the dandelion, whose white parachuted seeds are irresistible fun to blow into the wind. Many of these plants can be used for adding flavour to foods, and in medicine, aromatherapy and dyes. The many different and unique flowers give us pleasure for their delicate and often breathtaking beauty in colour and form. They are the inspiration of artists and poets and are often symbols of romance, or have meanings attached to them through folklore, legend or superstition.

Water-lilies & Arums
pp. 174–75

Carnivorous Plants
pp. 175–76

Lilies
pp. 176–77

Irises & Orchids
p. 178

Buttercups
pp. 179–80

Rose Family
pp. 180–81

Bunchberry
p. 181

Pea Family
pp. 181–83

Violet
p. 183

Flax
p. 184

Harebell
p. 184

Dogbane
p. 184

Milkweed
p. 185

Loosestrife
p. 185

Evening-Primrose
pp. 185–86

St. John's-wort
p. 186

Snapdragons
pp. 186–87

Touch-me-not
p. 187

Wintergreen
p. 187

Nettle
p. 188

Bergamot
p. 188

Teasel
p. 188

Aster Family
pp. 189–93

Carrot Family
p. 194

Bedstraw
p. 194

Dock
p. 195

Plantains
p. 196

Grasses & Cattails
p. 196

Ferns & Horsetails
p. 197

Yellow Pond-lily

Nuphar lutea

Leaves: 7–35 cm long, floating, heart-shaped
Flowers: 3.5–6 cm across, yellow, solitary
Fruit: spongy berries, 2–4.5 cm across

This floating, aquatic perennial grows from a large, buried rootstock. Some Native groups sliced the rootstocks and then ate them fried or boiled, or dried and ground them into flour, but other groups considered them inedible. If eaten in large amounts, pond-lily rootstocks can be potentially poisonous. Dried, sliced rootstocks were made into medicinal teas and used to treat arthritis, headaches, sore throats, heart problems or to aid in childbirth. **Where found:** still waters; throughout Ontario. **Also known as:** *N. variegata.*

White Water-lily

Nymphaea odorata

Leaves: 10–30 cm long, floating,
round with a V-shaped notch
Flowers: 7–20 cm across, white, solitary
Fruit: spongy berries

The pure white petals of this beautiful water-lily open in the morning and close by early afternoon. The fragrant flowers bloom throughout summer, making this plant a popular choice for water gardens. Individual flowers bloom for 4–5 days, long enough for pollination, and then sink underwater, where a berry develops. When mature, the fruit floats to the surface and slowly releases hundreds of tiny seeds. • Traditionally, the dried seeds were ground into flour or boiled into medicinal tea. **Where found:** still waters; southern ²⁄₃ of Ontario.

Skunk Cabbage

Symplocarpus foetidus

Height: up to 55 cm
Leaves: 40–55 cm long
Flowers: tiny, clustered on a ball-like spathe inside a hooded
spadix 10–15 cm high
Fruit: brown-black berries, in rounded clusters

Skunk cabbage is a foul-smelling, wetland plant that emits a mild odour when left alone but is especially pungent when damaged. The smell attracts carrion-feeding and other pollinating insects but repels animals that may eat or otherwise damage the plant. • Skunk cabbage is one of the few plants that can produce heat through cellular respiration. This incredible plant can even melt frozen ground by warming its surroundings 15–35°C above the air temperature. **Where found:** wetlands; southern ½ of Ontario.

Jack-in-the-pulpit

Arisaema triphyllum

Height: up to 65 cm
Leaves: 2 leaves, each divided into 3 leaflets 8–15 cm long
Flowers: tiny, clustered on a spadix 8 cm long
Fruit: smooth, shiny, green berries (red at maturity)

Unusual jack-in-the-pulpit flowers are composed of a spadix (jack) covered with tiny male and female flowers which is surrounded by a green-and-purple-streaked spathe (pulpit). One or two basal leaves, each divided into 3 leaflets, overshadow the flower. • The entire plant and the bright red berries are poisonous if eaten fresh, but Native peoples pounded the dried roots into flour and used jack-in-the-pulpit in cough and cold remedies. Various birds eat the berries, including wild turkey and ring-necked pheasant. **Where found:** moist hardwood forests; southern ½ of Ontario.

Pitcher-plant

Sarracenia purpurea

Height: 20–40 cm
Leaves: 10–30 cm long, basal, often water-filled
Flowers: 5–7 cm across, purplish red, solitary, nodding
Fruit: capsules

The unusual pitcher-plant is our largest carnivorous plant. The colourful, hood-like lips of the hollow leaves (pitchers) attract insects and draw them inward. The slippery inner surface of the pitcher is covered in stiff, downward-pointing hairs, making it impossible for visitors to retreat. Eventually the insect falls into the liquid at the bottom of the cup, drowns and is digested by the plant. • Pitcher-plant was highly regarded and was used medicinally by Native peoples. **Where found:** bogs, fens and muskeg; throughout Ontario.

Common Bladderwort

Utricularia vulgaris

Stem length: 1 m or more
Leaves: 1–5 cm long, divided into many thread-like segments
Flowers: 1.2–2 cm long, bright yellow
Fruit: capsules

Most carnivorous plants trap and eat insects, but aquatic bladderworts digest everything from tiny worms to small crustaceans. Like other carnivorous plants, bladderworts are typically found in cold, acidic, nitrogen-poor environments. These plants get their nitrogen from the invertebrates they digest, so they are able to grow where others cannot survive. • Several bladderwort species are found in Ontario. They float on water or creep along muddy shores, with upright flower stalks growing above the water. **Where found:** shallow to deep water; throughout Ontario to treeline.

Sundew
Drosera rotundifolia

Height: 5–18 cm
Leaves: 4–10 mm across, round, basal, on flattened stalks 3–6 cm long
Flowers: 4–6 mm across, pink to white
Fruit: capsules, 5–7 mm across

This insect-eating plant has round leaves covered in sticky, reddish "tentacles" (hairs) ideal for attracting, trapping and digesting prey. The gland-tipped tentacles curl around a victim, then secrete an enzyme that dissolves the prey within 48 hours, leaving only the exoskeleton. • Sundew has been used to treat respiratory problems and was made into love potions. Some farmers in the 19th century believed that "sheep and other cattell, if they do but taste [sundew], are provoked to lust." **Where found:** sphagnum bogs, fens and swamps; throughout Ontario to treeline.

Wood Lily
Lilium philadelphicum

Height: 30–90 cm
Leaves: 3–10 cm long, in whorls of 3–8
Flowers: 6–10 cm across, reddish orange, erect
Fruit: capsules, 1–2 cm long

Bright, showy wood lilies spring up along roadsides and in woodlands across much of Canada. • Native peoples ate the peppery bulbs, tiny tubers and flowers raw or cooked. The bulbs were used in poultices to heal wounds, heart problems and toothaches, or they were steeped into a tea that was used to treat fevers or wash sores. • Unfortunately, wood lilies no longer grow in many areas because picking the flowers or gathering the roots kills the entire plant. Please leave wood lilies where they are so that others may enjoy them. **Where found:** roadsides, dry woods, meadows; southern ⅔ of Ontario.

White Trillium
Trillium grandiflorum

Height: 20–40 cm
Leaves: 8–15 cm long, in a whorl of 3
Flowers: 5–10 cm across, white, 3 petals
Fruit: red berries, 1 cm across

The beautiful white trillium became Ontario's floral emblem in 1937. Trilliums carpet the ground in shady deciduous forests, but flowers do not appear until plants are at least 6 years old. • When the ripe fruits split open, many sticky seeds are revealed. The seeds contain special oily bodies called elaiosomes, which are as tasty as potato chips to ants. The ants carry the seeds to their nests and bite off the "ant snack," leaving the seed to grow far from the parent plant. **Where found:** rich woodlands; southeastern ⅓ of Ontario. **Also known as:** snow trillium.

White Death-camas

Zigadenus elegans

Height: 20–60 cm
Leaves: 10–20 cm long, narrow
Flowers: 1–2 cm across, greenish white, in open clusters
Fruit: erect, 3-lobed capsules, 1.5 cm across

This perennial contains the poisonous alkaloid zygadenine, which some people claim is more potent than strychnine. Death-camas has been confused with wild onions, blue camas, white hyacinth and fritillarias, with disastrous results. When in doubt, spit it out! If ingested, induce vomiting and get medical help. • Growing from blackish-scaly bulbs, this plant has pale, foul-smelling flowers, each with 6 greenish, heart-shaped glands near the centre. **Where found:** moist, open sites; southeastern ⅓ of Ontario.

Wild Lily-of-the-valley

Maianthemum canadense

Height: 15 cm
Leaves: 2–8 cm long, 2 (occasionally 3)
Flowers: 4–6 mm across, white, star-shaped, in erect clusters
Fruit: brownish green berries (red at maturity), 3–4 mm across

This small understorey herb can be recognized by its parallel-veined, heart-shaped leaves. Native peoples used the leaves to promote healing, placing fresh leaves directly on a cut. Crushed leaves were also applied to reduce swelling, and a concoction of dried, boiled leaves was used to soak wounds. • Although the berries are edible, their numbers are limited, taste unremarkable and eating too many can cause diarrhea. **Where found:** moist woodlands; throughout the southern ¾ of Ontario.

Star-flowered Solomon's-seal

Maianthemum stellatum

Height: 15–60 cm
Leaves: 3–12 cm long, lance-shaped
Flowers: <1 cm across, white, star-shaped, in erect clusters
Fruit: berries, 0.6–1 cm across

The species name *stellata,* from the Latin *stella,* meaning "star," aptly describes the radiant, white flowers of this woodland wildflower. The unbranched, slightly arching plants produce clusters of dark blue or reddish black berries, which are greenish yellow with purplish stripes when young. • A larger relative, false Solomon's-seal (*M. racemosum; Smilacina racemosa*) is easily recognized by its 5–15-cm, puffy, pyramidal flower clusters and its wavy-edged (rather than straight-edged) leaves. **Where found:** moist to dry sites; throughout much of Ontario, except the northwest. **Also known as:** *S. stellata.*

Northern Blue Flag

Iris versicolor

Height: 20–80 cm
Leaves: 10–80 cm long, 1.3–2.5 cm wide, basal
Flowers: 3 purple-blue sepals 4–7 cm long, white near the base and with a yellow spot; 3 purple-blue petals 2–4.5 cm long
Fruit: beaked, oblong capsules

There are hundreds of colourful iris species, named for the Greek goddess of the rainbow. The 3 parts of this showy flower symbolize wisdom, faith and courage. Our native species, northern blue flag, blooms from May to July. • This plant's highly poisonous roots and shoots can cause difficulty breathing, upset stomach and diarrhea if eaten. Handling this plant can cause severe skin rashes in some people. **Where found:** wet sites; throughout Ontario.

Common Blue-eyed-grass

Sisyrinchium montanum

Height: 10–50 cm
Leaves: basal, 2–6 cm long, narrow
Flowers: purple-blue, 1.5–3 cm across
Fruit: round capsules, 3–6 mm across

The dainty blue blossoms of this wildflower add fleeting beauty to damp meadows and woodland trails. Common blue-eyed-grass is not a true grass but a member of the iris family. If you compare the stems, you'll find that the stems of these plants are flat, whereas grass stems are round. • Dozens of blue-eyed-grass species are found around the world, but some have white, yellow or purple flowers. **Where found:** moist, open areas; throughout Ontario.

Yellow Lady's-slipper

Cypripedium parviflorum

Height: 10–70 cm
Leaves: to 20 cm long, 1.5–14 cm wide
Flowers: 4 twisted petals around a yellow, 3.5 cm long, sac-like pouch
Fruit: oblong capsules

Finding a patch of these uncommon orchids is a treat. They depend on special mycorrhizal fungi for nutrient intake, water absorption and seed growth. Do not transplant these unusual orchids to your garden as they will likely not survive without the fungi. Wild orchids are rare because of habitat loss and overharvesting. The sac-like flowers trap insects, which slide down their slippery walls and must climb out past the pollen-laden stigma. **Where found:** moist hardwood or mixedwood forests and bogs; throughout Ontario. **Also known as:** *C. calceolus*.

Tall Meadowrue

Thalictrum dasycarpum

Height: 1–2 m
Leaves: divided 3–4 times into groups of 3 leaflets
Flowers: 1.5–3.5 mm long, pale yellow to purple, in clusters
Fruit: seed-like achenes, 4–6 mm across

When tall meadowrue blooms, it is hard to miss. The tiny flowers appear in showy, pyramid-shaped clusters. • Plants are usually either male or female. Male flowers have dangling stamens, and the less showy female flowers give way to small fruit. • Dried seeds and leaves may be used as a fragrant potpourri. Some Native peoples used this plant in love potions. **Where found:** wet, open sites; southern ¾ of Ontario.

Red Baneberry

Actaea rubra

Height: 30–100 cm
Leaves: divided 2–3 times into groups of 3 leaflets
Flowers: 7 mm across, white
Fruit: glossy, red or white berries, 6–8 mm long

This perennial has long-stalked, rounded clusters of white flowers, each with 5–10 tiny, slender petals. Although birds and small mammals eat the tempting fruit, baneberry is toxic to humans. As few as 2 berries can cause cramps, headaches, vomiting, bloody diarrhea and/or dizziness. • Some Native peoples considered baneberry to be sacred and used it in religious ceremonies, but this plant was always treated with respect, because it could kill the user. **Where found:** moist, often shady sites; throughout Ontario.

Meadow Buttercup

Ranunculus acris

Height: 60–100 cm
Leaves: to 10 cm wide, deeply palmately divided
Flowers: 2.5 cm across, yellow, 5 petals
Fruit: seed-like achenes, 2–3 mm across

Buttercups get their genus name from the toxic ranunculin contained in their sap. It causes symptoms that include dermatitis, mouth blisters and intense burning pain of the digestive tract when ingested. Drying and cooking are said to degrade the poison, rendering plants or hay that contain buttercups harmless. • Traditionally, the sap was applied to warts or plague sores, and the juice was used to irritate the skin to counteract arthritis and nerve pain. **Where found:** disturbed ground and fields; southern ¾ of Ontario.

Yellow Marsh-marigold

Caltha palustris

Height: 20–60 cm
Leaves: 5–17 cm long, heart- or kidney-shaped, toothed
Flowers: 1.5–4 cm across, yellow, 5–9 petal-like sepals
Fruit: capsules, 1–1.5 cm long

These bright yellow, saucer-shaped flowers may be overlooked because they grow along the banks of ponds and in shady, damp places. To humans, these flowers look evenly yellow, but insects can detect distinct ultraviolet light patterns along the "petals" that guide them to the centre of the flower. • The raw leaves contain a toxin that can irritate skin and is poisonous if eaten. **Where found:** wet sites, near or in shallow water; throughout Ontario.

Canada Anemone

Anemone canadensis

Height: 20–70 cm
Leaves: 5–15 cm long, divided into 3–5 toothed segments
Flowers: 2–4 cm across, white
Fruit: seed-like achenes, 3–5 mm across, in round heads

Beautiful, delicate Canada anemone flowers bloom in June and July, unfolding above unique, deeply lobed leaves. The flowers do not have true petals, but 5 showy, petal-like sepals. Small, green seed clusters (achenes) appear after the blooms fade. • Some Native peoples used the roots and leaves in poultices to clean or heal sores, cuts and nosebleeds, but this plant contains caustic substances that may irritate the skin. **Where found:** dry, open sites, roadsides, gravely shores; throughout Ontario. **Also known as:** windflower.

Common Silverweed

Argentina anserina

Height: low, creeping
Leaves: to 30 cm long, divided into numerous toothed leaflets
Flowers: 1.5–2.5 cm across, yellow, 5 petals
Fruit: achenes, 2 mm across

This circumpolar plant carpets the ground with its sharply toothed leaflets and bright yellow flowers. The leaves, especially the undersides, are covered in silky, silver hairs, from which the plant gets its name. • Silverweed roots may be eaten raw or cooked and are said to taste like parsnips or sweet potatoes. Ground roots were traditionally steeped into medicinal tea, which was used to aid in childbirth or treat diarrhea. **Where found:** well-drained to wet, open sites including meadows, ditches and riversides; throughout Ontario. **Also known as:** *Potentilla anserina.*

Wild Strawberry

Fragaria virginiana

Height: 5–15 cm
Leaves: 5–10 cm long, divided into 3 coarsely toothed leaflets
Flowers: 1.5–2 cm across, white, 5 petals
Fruit: strawberry, <1 cm across

This inconspicuous little plant is the ancestor of 90% of our cultivated strawberries. Each tiny, red berry contains all the flavour of a large domestic strawberry. • The rhizomes and runners produce tufts of bluish-tinged leaves with 3-toothed leaflets. • Native peoples enjoyed strawberries fresh or dried for winter use. • Woodland strawberry (*F. vesca*) has yellow-green leaflets with the end tooth projecting beyond adjacent teeth; the end tooth is shorter in wild strawberry. **Where found:** well-drained, open sites; throughout Ontario. **Also known as:** common strawberry.

Bunchberry

Cornus canadensis

Height: 5–20 cm
Leaves: 2–8 cm long, deeply veined, in a whorl of 4–6
Flowers: tiny, in a cluster of 5–15, surrounded by 4 white, petal-like bracts
Fruit: round drupes, red, 6–8 mm across

These small flowers are really miniature bouquets of tiny blooms surrounded by showy bracts. The true flowers, at the centre, are easily overlooked. The large, white bracts attract insects and provide good landing platforms. • The berry-like drupes are edible, raw or cooked. They are not very flavourful, but the crunchy, poppy-like seeds are enjoyable. **Where found:** dry to moist sites; throughout Ontario.

American Vetch

Vicia americana

Height: 20–120 cm
Leaves: compound, divided into 8–14 leaflets, each 1.5–3.5 cm long, tipped with a tendril
Flowers: 1.5–2 cm lone, bluish purple, pea-like
Fruit: pods, 2–3 cm long

Twining tendrils wrap around nearby stems and leaves as this slender vine climbs upward over its neighbours. Its flat, hairless "pea pods" are attractive to young children, but they are not edible. • When an insect lands on a vetch flower, anthers spring out to dust the insect's belly with pollen. The next flower collects the pollen on its stigma and applies another load of pollen. **Where found:** moist, fairly open sites; throughout Ontario.

Bigleaf Lupine

Lupinus polyphyllus

Height: 50–150 cm
Leaves: 4–13 cm long, divided into 10–24 leaflets, tipped with a tendril
Flowers: 1.2–1.6 cm long, purple-blue, pea-like, in 1-sided clusters
Fruit: pods, 3–5 cm long

This attractive perennial, with its showy flower clusters and fuzzy seed pods, enriches the soil with nitrogen. • The seed pods look like hairy garden peas, and children may incorrectly assume that they are edible. Many lupines contain poisonous alkaloids, and it is difficult to distinguish between poisonous and non-poisonous species. • The pea-like flowers have silky upper sides and form loose clusters, 20–40 cm long. **Where found:** moderately dry, open sites; southern ⅔ of Ontario.

Alfalfa

Medicago sativa

Height: up to 1 m
Leaves: divided into 3 leaflets, each 1.5–3 cm long, toothed at the tip
Flowers: 6–12 mm long, purple-blue, pea-like, in rounded clusters
Fruit: small, curved or coiled pods

Alfalfa is an important forage crop that grows in a wide range of agricultural regions. Native to Iran, alfalfa was cultivated as horse feed in Greece as early as 490 BC, then imported to South America by the Spaniards. Today, this legume is harvested as hay and often used to feed cattle. Tasty, young alfalfa sprouts are also sold as salad and sandwich garnish. • The name "alfalfa" is derived from the Arabic *al-fasfasah*, meaning "best fodder." **Where found:** disturbed sites; throughout Ontario.

Sweet-clover

Melilotus officinalis

Height: 50–200 cm
Leaves: divided into 3 leaflets, each 1–2.5 cm long, lance-shaped, toothed
Flowers: 4.5–7 mm long, yellow, pea-like, in long, narrow clusters
Fruit: pods, 3 mm long

This hardy forage crop blankets roadsides and abandoned fields in yellow, invading native grasslands and reducing diversity. Each pollinated plant can release as many as 350,000 seeds that remain viable for decades. • Sweet-clover is valued as a forage crop, soil enhancer and a honey plant. The genus name stems from *meli*, Greek for "honey," and refers to this plant's abundant, nectar-producing flowers. • White-flowered sweet-clover is known as *M. alba*. **Where found:** open, disturbed sites; throughout Ontario.

Alsike Clover

Trifolium hybridum

Height: 30–80 cm
Leaves: divided into 3 leaflets, each 1.5–5 cm long
Flowers: 7–10 mm long, white or pinkish, in dense clusters
Fruit: tiny pods

Clover has long been cultivated as a fodder because it grows quickly in a wide range of soils and locations and makes a nutritious, protein-rich livestock feed. Alsike clover also adds nitrogen to poor soils and stabilizes roadsides. • What most people call the "flower" is actually a cluster of many tiny, tubular blossoms. • Fresh or dried flower heads may be added to soups or stews, but clovers are hard to digest and may cause bloating. Traditionally, they were only eaten if other food was scarce. **Where found:** disturbed sites; throughout Ontario.

Red Clover

Trifolium pratense

Height: 80 cm
Leaves: divided into 3 leaflets, each 2–5 cm long
Flowers: 1.5–2 cm long, pink to purple, in dense heads
Fruit: 1-seeded pods

Red clover has round flower heads and large leaves. • Native to Europe, clover is widely used around the world as fodder. It is dependent on bumble bees for pollination, so when clover crops were introduced to Australia, bumble bees were imported, too. • Medicinally, red clover has been used as a blood purifier, cough remedy and treatment for eczema. It should not be consumed in autumn, when the level of toxins in the plants increases. **Where found:** disturbed sites; throughout Ontario.

Early Blue Violet

Viola adunca

Height: 5–10 cm
Leaves: 1–3 cm long, heart-shaped
Flowers: 1–1.5 cm across, purple to blue, white throat
Fruit: capsules, 4 mm long

Few of these dainty, blue to violet flowers are fertilized each spring. When no seed is produced, small, inconspicuous blooms appear in autumn, hidden away among debris near ground level. These never open and, instead, fertilize themselves, producing abundant, fast-growing seeds. Flowers that are fertilized develop into capsules that burst open, explosively shooting out seeds. • Canada violet (*V. canadensis*) has leafy stems 10–40 cm tall, broad, heart-shaped leaves and whitish flowers with fine, purple lines. **Where found:** dry to moist sites; southern ½ of Ontario.

Cultivated Flax

Linum usitatissimum

Height: 30–90 cm
Leaves: 1.5–3.5 cm long, lance-shaped
Flowers: 2–3 cm across, blue, 5 petals
Fruit: round capsules

The beautiful, delicate, pale to sky blue blossoms of flax usually open in the morning and fade in the hot sun later the same day. Most plants produce only one flower at a time, with the next bud opening the following morning. • The stems contain long, tough fibres, which have been used to make ropes, cords, fishing lines and nets. The ground seeds are high in fibre and make a tasty addition to breads or other baked goods. Bright yellow flaxseed oil can be used to lower cholesterol or treat sore throats, arthritis and skin irritations. **Where found:** dry, open sites.

Harebell

Campanula rotundifolia

Height: 10–50 cm
Leaves: 1–6 cm long; stem leaves narrow; basal leaves rounded
Flowers: 2 cm long, purple-blue, bell-shaped
Fruit: capsules, 5–8 mm long

From open woodlands to exposed, rocky slopes, these delicate, nodding bells bob in the breeze on thin, wiry stems. • The small openings at the base of the capsules close quickly in damp weather, protecting the seeds from excess moisture. On dry, windy days, the capsules swing widely in the breeze, scattering the seeds. • The species name *rotundifolia* refers to this plant's round, basal leaves. **Where found:** moist to dry, open sites; throughout Ontario.

Spreading Dogbane

Apocynum androsaemifolium

Height: 20–70 cm
Leaves: 2–10 cm long, drooping, in pairs
Flowers: 0.4–1.2 cm across, pink, bell-shaped
Fruit: hanging pods, 5–15 cm long

These delicate, innocent-looking flowers can be death traps. Toothed scales on the petals spring inward when touched, catching the mouthparts of unsuspecting insects. Butterflies and bees may free themselves, but smaller insects remain trapped and die. • Native peoples rolled the tough stem fibres into fine thread and plaited strands to make bowstrings, cord and nets. • This perennial has milky sap. Each sweet-scented flower produces a hanging pair of slender pods that split down one side to release tiny seeds with silky parachutes. **Where found:** well-drained, open sites; throughout the southern ¾ of Ontario.

Common Milkweed

Asclepias syriaca

Height: 50–150 cm
Leaves: 10–20 cm long, in pairs
Flowers: 8–12 mm across, pink to purplish, in rounded clusters
Fruit: woolly pods, 7–12 cm long

Common milkweed grows in large colonies, connected by underground runners that sprout new shoots each year. • This plant contains glycosides that are toxic to animals and humans, but some insects depend on milkweed to survive, including monarch butterflies and several milkweed beetles. Monarch butterfly larvae feed solely on milkweed leaves, absorbing the toxic glycosides into their bodies so that both larvae and adult butterflies become poisonous to predators. **Where found:** open, disturbed areas in southern ½ of Ontario.

Purple Loosestrife

Lythrum salicaria

Height: 50–150 cm
Leaves: 3–10 cm long, in pairs or 3s
Flowers: 1–2 cm across, pink-purple, in spike-like clusters
Fruit: small capsules

Since its introduction to North America 200 years ago, purple loosestrife has spread across the continent. This aggressive weed turns wetland communities into silent monocultures by smothering native plants. Creeping rootstocks and prolific seeds (up to 2 million per plant) enable this "silent killer" to spread rapidly. The natural predators and diseases that regulate purple loosestrife in Eurasia do not exist here, so this plant thrives unmolested. Control methods include digging out and burning plants or removing and burning seed and flower heads. **Where found:** wet sites; southern ⅔ of Ontario.

Common Fireweed

Chamerion angustifolium

Height: 30–300 cm
Leaves: 2–20 cm long, lance-shaped
Flowers: 2–4 cm across, pink-purple, in spike-like clusters
Fruit: pods, 4–8 cm long

Fireweed helps heal landscape scars such as roadsides and burned forests by blanketing the ground with colonies of plants, often producing a sea of deep pink flowers. • Young shoots can be eaten like asparagus, and the flowers can be added to salads. • Hairy willow-herb (*Epilobium hirsutum*) is 50–200 cm tall, with sharply toothed leaves and purplish pink flowers, 2.5 cm wide, in spike-like clusters. **Where found:** open, often disturbed sites; throughout Ontario. **Also known as:** *E. angustifolium.*

Common Evening-primrose

Oenothera biennis

Height: 50–150 cm
Leaves: 10–20 cm long, lance-shaped
Flowers: 2.5–5 cm across, yellow, in leafy clusters
Fruit: capsules, 1.5–4 cm long

Evening-primrose is best known for its abundant, oil-rich seeds, which contain essential fatty acids. The seeds are processed into evening-primrose oil, which can be used to treat eczema, high cholesterol, heart disease, PMS, asthma, arthritis and many other ailments. The seeds and flowers may be eaten in salads, and young leaves or flowers may be steamed as greens. The roots have been likened to parsnips and may be sliced, fried and added to soups or stews. **Where found:** dry, open sites; southern ¾ of Ontario.

Common St. John's-wort

Hypericum perforatum

Height: 30–80 cm
Leaves: 1–4 cm long, paired, with translucent dots
Flowers: 2 cm across, yellow, 5 petals with black dots on the edges
Fruit: capsules, 7–8 mm long

Common St. John's-wort is a well-known medicinal herb that has become a troublesome, fast-spreading weed in some areas. • Teas, washes and lotions made from this plant have been used to treat a variety of ailments from wounds and sore joints to insomnia, anxiety and stomach ulcers. Glandular dots on the flowers and leaves contain hypericin, an enzyme inhibitor with antidepressant and antiviral properties. This phototoxin can cause skin reactions in humans and light-coloured farm animals. **Where found:** disturbed sites; southern ⅔ of Ontario.

Great Mullein

Verbascum thapsus

Height: 1–2 m
Leaves: 30 cm long, thick, felted
Flowers: 1–2.5 cm across, yellow, in spikes 20–50 cm long
Fruit: 2-parted capsules

Great mullein was introduced to North America from Europe in the 18th century as a medicinal herb. Since each plant can produce 150,000 minute seeds and most flowers can self-fertilize, it soon became an abundant, naturalized weed. • In Europe, dried stems were used for lamp wicks or dipped in suet to make torches, which were believed to drive away witches and evil spirits. This important medicinal plant was used to remedy many conditions, including spasmodic coughs, fevers, diarrhea and hemorrhoids. **Where found:** disturbed sites; southern ⅔ of Ontario.

Butter-and-eggs

Linaria vulgaris

Height: 30–80 cm
Leaves: 2–6 cm long, narrow
Flowers: 2–3.5 cm long, snapdragon-like, yellow, lower lip orange
Fruit: capsules, 8–12 mm long

This native of Eurasia spreads rapidly by both hardy, creeping roots and seed. It makes an attractive ornamental, but can be difficult to remove from your garden. Cut flowers are quite resilient and last long in a vase. • Most animals avoid this pungent and potentially toxic plant, but large pollinating insects appreciate its abundant flowers. To access nectar, insects must be strong enough to pry apart the snapdragon-like flowers. **Where found:** disturbed sites. **Also known as:** toadflax.

Spotted Touch-me-not

Impatiens capensis

Height: 50–150 cm
Leaves: 3–10 cm long, toothed, thin
Flowers: 2–2.5 cm long, orange with brown spots, funnel-shaped
Fruit: pods, 2 cm long

The beautiful, golden orange flowers of spotted touch-me-not are the perfect shape for attracting hummingbirds. Since the dangling flowers look a bit like jewelled earrings, this plant is also called jewelweed. • The leaves have long been used by Native peoples and herbalists to treat rashes caused by poison ivy, poison oak and stinging nettle. Poultices made from leaf or stem extracts are said to counteract a variety of skin ailments including dermatitis, insect bites and warts. **Where found:** moist, open forests; southern ¾ of Ontario. **Also known as:** jewelweed.

Common Pink Wintergreen

Pyrola asarifolia

Height: 10–30 cm
Leaves: 2–6 cm long, rounded, leathery, in a basal rosette
Flowers: 0.8–1.2 cm across, pink, bell-shaped, nodding
Fruit: round capsules, 5–10 mm across

Wintergreens grow in intimate association with soil fungi (mycorrhizae). Some species produce all of their food by photosynthesis, but others take their food almost entirely from dead organic matter via these fungi. Mycorrhizae are unlikely to be found in a garden environment, so these plants should not be transplanted. **Where found:** moist, often shady sites; throughout Ontario. **Also known as:** pink pyrola.

Stinging Nettle

Urtica dioica

Height: 0.5–2 m
Leaves: 4–15 cm long, coarsely toothed
Flowers: 1–2 mm long, green to purplish, in drooping clusters
Fruit: achenes, 1–2 mm long

The stinging hairs on the stems and undersides of this plant's leaves contain formic acid and can cause itching and burning. The sting lasts 10 minutes to several days, depending on how sensitive you are. • Some people use gloves to pick young, tender nettles to make soup or steam them as a delicious spring vegetable. Cooking destroys the acid but eating large amounts may cause irritation. **Where found:** moist, rich meadows, ditches, woodlands and disturbed sites; throughout Ontario.

Wild Bergamot

Monarda fistulosa

Height: 20–70 cm
Leaves: 2.5–8 cm, toothed
Flowers: 2–3.5 cm long, purple to pink; in heads 1–3.5 cm wide
Fruit: 4 nutlets

Wild bergamot's long, tubular, rose to purplish flowers attract hummingbirds and hawk moths. • This plant provides a spice, potherb and tea (similar to Earl Grey). Native peoples used the tea to treat ailments ranging from colds and indigestion to pneumonia and kidney problems. Dried leaves were burned or sprinkled on items to repel insects. • This showy, aromatic perennial can also be grown from seed (smooth nutlets) in gardens. **Where found:** moist to moderately dry, open sites; southern ¾ of Ontario. **Also known as:** horsemint.

Wild Purple Teasel

Dipsacus fullonum

Height: up to 2 m
Leaves: 10–40 cm long, in pairs
Flowers: 10–15 mm across, pink to purple; in dense, egg-shaped heads
Fruit: achenes

This plant was introduced from Africa and Eurasia. The interesting-looking, oval flower clusters have long, prickly bracts protruding from the base. Tiny purple flowers form a ring around the flower head. • Both the common name "teasel" and the species name *fullonum* refer to the hooked bracts on the heads of a related cultivar that was once used to "tease" or "full out" wool fibres in cloth making. **Where found:** disturbed sites in the southeastern ⅓ of Ontario.

Spotted Knapweed

Centaurea biebersteinii

Height: 30–100 cm
Leaves: 2.5–6 cm long, divided into narrow lobes
Flowers: disk flowers pink to purple; in heads 2–2.5 cm across
Fruit: seed-like achenes

Spotted knapweed is an aggressive, noxious weed that spreads rapidly through agricultural land, affecting crop yield. The first Canadian report came from Victoria, BC, in 1893, and 40 years later, it had spread across the country to Québec. Each plant can produce thousands of seeds that remain viable for 5 or more years. Once seeded, knapweed grows earlier in the season than other plants, allowing it to outcompete crops for water, sunlight and nutrients. **Where found:** disturbed sites; throughout Ontario. **Also known as:** *C. maculosa*.

Canada Thistle

Cirsium arvense

Height: 30–150 cm
Leaves: 5–15 cm long, spiny-toothed
Flowers: disk flowers pink-purple; in heads 1.5–2.5 cm across
Fruit: seed-like achenes

Canada thistle was introduced to Canada from Europe in the 17th century. Today this aggressive weed is found in virtually all crop-lands and pastures. Prickly thistle colonies choke out other plants, reducing crop yields, and grow from deep underground runners that produce a substance that inhibits the growth of nearby plants. Each year, one plant can send out up to 6 m of runners, and female plants can release up to 40,000 seeds. • These plants can be beneficial. The flowers provide a good source of pollen and nectar for honey bees, and humans can eat the shoots and roots. **Where found:** disturbed sites; southern ½ of Ontario.

Bull Thistle

Cirsium vulgare

Height: 50–150 cm
Leaves: 7–15 cm long, spiny-toothed
Flowers: disk flowers purplish; in heads 4–5 cm across
Fruit: seed-like achenes

This spiny thistle was introduced from Europe and now grows freely throughout North America. • Almost all parts of this plant are edible once the sharp spines have been removed. The leaves, stems and roots of first-year plants can be eaten raw or steamed. • American goldfinches delight in perching on late-summer thistle heads. These birds line their nests with the fluffy thistledown, and thistle seeds provide an important source of food for their young. **Where found:** disturbed sites; southern ½ of Ontario.

Chicory

Cichorium intybus

Height: 30–120 cm
Leaves: 8–20 cm long, mostly basal, becoming smaller up the stem
Flowers: ray flowers blue or white, toothed; in heads 2–4 cm across
Fruit: seed-like achenes, 2–3 mm across

Introduced to Canada from Europe, chicory is a common roadside weed with bluish flower heads and a long taproot. It can be used as a coffee substitute or coffee additive. The young green leaves and edible flowers can be added to salads. • Cultivated chicory, known as Belgian endive or radicchio, and true endive (*C. endivia*) are grown under special, dark conditions so that the leaves remain tender. **Where found:** disturbed ground; southern ½ of Ontario.

Common Dandelion

Taraxacum officinale

Height: 5–50 cm
Leaves: 5–40 cm long, basal, deeply lobed
Flowers: ray flowers yellow; in solitary heads 2–5 cm across
Fruit: seed-like achenes

Common dandelion is not a popular plant, but it has been receiving some positive press lately for its vitamin-rich leaves. This plant was originally brought to North America from Eurasia, where it was cultivated for food and medicine. Young dandelion leaves and flower heads are chock full of vitamins and minerals and make nutritious additions to salads. They may be served as cooked vegetables or added to pancakes, muffins or fritters, or even made into wine. The roots can be ground into a caffeine-free coffee substitute or boiled to make a red dye. **Where found:** disturbed sites; throughout Ontario.

Yellow Hawkweed

Hieracium caespitosum

Height: 25–90 cm
Leaves: 5–25 cm long, basal, spatula-shaped
Flowers: ray flowers yellow; in heads 1–2 cm across
Fruit: cylindrical, seed-like achenes

Yellow hawkweed and its cousin, orange hawkweed (*H. aurantiacum*), are common wayside weeds that spread easily by underground runners and seeds. The showy flower heads of these plants attract insects, but fertilization is rare. Most offspring grow from the runners and are genetically identical to the parent plant. • Hawkweed's milky sap contains rubbery latex, and Native peoples chewed the leaves of these plants like gum. • Orange hawkweed is 10–60 cm tall with leaves 5–15 cm long and compact, red-orange flowers. **Where found:** moist to wet, open sites; southern ¾ of Ontario. **Also known as:** king devil, meadow hawkweed.

Perennial Sow-thistle

Sonchus arvensis

Height: 40–200 cm
Leaves: 5–40 cm long, deeply lobed, prickly edges
Flowers: ray flowers yellow; in heads 3–5 cm across
Fruit: achenes, 2.5–3.5 mm across

Tall perennial sow-thistle is something like a dandelion on steroids, growing taller and faster than neighbouring plants. Hardy roots and abundant seeds help it to spread rapidly, outcompeting crops for moisture, nutrients and sunlight. • The young leaves taste similar to lettuce and may be used in salads, along with the edible flower heads. Older leaves can be cooked as a vegetable. • This plant is devoured by livestock and rabbits and is a host plant for aphids. **Where found:** disturbed sites in the southern ⅔ of Ontario. **Also known as:** field sow-thistle, hare thistle, hare lettuce.

Oxeye Daisy

Leucanthemum vulgare

Height: 20–90 cm
Leaves: 4–15 cm long, deeply lobed, becoming smaller up the stem
Flowers: ray flowers white, 15–35; disk flowers yellow; in heads 2.5–5 cm across
Fruit: seed-like achenes

A favourite among children, daisies can be braided into necklaces and crowns or plucked apart to the verse "He loves me, he loves me not." • Oxeye daisies were introduced from Eurasia 400 years ago and now carpet fields, ditches and abandoned lots across North America. Despite being a common weed that competes against native plants and crops, daisies are often depicted as cheerful, welcome additions to gardens. • The shasta daisy (*Chrysanthemum maximum*) is a larger, more robust ornamental variety. **Where found:** open, disturbed area; southern ¾ of Ontario.

Black-eyed Susan

Rudbeckia hirta

Height: 30–100 cm
Leaves: 5–17 cm long, lance-shaped
Flowers: ray flowers yellow-orange, 8–20; disk flowers purple-brown, dome-shaped; in heads 5–10 cm across
Fruit: seed-like achenes

Native to central North America, cheerful black-eyed Susans have spread from coast to coast over the last century. • Medicinally, this plant was taken internally to increase urination or expel worms. It was also used in a wash to soothe snakebites and wounds. Black-eyed Susan poultices were rubbed on horses' saddle sores to aid healing. **Where found:** open, disturbed ground; southern ½ of Ontario. **Also known as:** *R. serotina*.

Fringed Aster

Symphyotrichum ciliolatum

Height: 20–120 cm
Leaves: 4–12 cm long
Flowers: ray flowers, purple-blue; disk flowers yellow; in heads 1.5–3 cm across
Fruit: seed-like achenes

These cheerful, purplish asters beautify many of Ontario's trails, clearings and roadsides. The large, heart-shaped lower leaves make fringed aster easy to identify. • Traditionally, the roots of this plant were boiled to treat pink eye or crushed and applied as a poultice to stop bleeding. • The name "aster" means "star" and refers to the shape of the flowers. **Where found:** open, disturbed areas and forests; throughout Ontario. **Also known as:** Lindley's aster; *Aster ciliolatus.*

Pineapple-weed

Matricaria discoidea

Height: 5–40 cm
Leaves: 1–5 cm long, fern-like
Flowers: disk flowers greenish yellow; in heads 5–9 mm across
Fruit: tiny achenes

Pineapple-weed is a close relative of chamomile and gives off a similar, pineapple-like aroma when crushed. • The young flower heads can be steeped into a soothing tea or eaten raw in salads. • Like closely related ragweed (*Ambrosia* spp.), pineapple-weed can cause allergic reactions in some people. Look for this common weed growing along sidewalks, roadsides or other areas with poor, compacted soil. **Where found:** open, disturbed sites; throughout Ontario.

Common Tansy

Tanacetum vulgare

Height: 40–100 cm
Leaves: 10–20 cm long, fern-like
Flowers: disk flowers yellow; in dense heads 5–10 mm across
Fruit: seed-like achenes

Yellow, button-like flowers top common tansy, a medicinal and horticultural herb introduced from Europe. This rapidly spreading weed is often found in ditches or along rivers, where the current carries the seeds downstream. • Tansy has been used medicinally to treat many ailments, including migraine headaches, jaundice and intestinal and bladder problems, but the volatile oils of this plant are toxic and potentially fatal. **Where found:** disturbed sites; southern ⅔ of Ontario.

Canada Goldenrod

Solidago canadensis

Height: 30–120 cm
Leaves: 5–10 cm long, lance-shaped
Flowers: ray and disk flowers tiny, yellow; in heads 5 mm across
Fruit: hairy achenes

Many people accuse these bold, pyramid-shaped flower clusters of causing hay fever, but the real culprit is probably a less conspicuous plant, such as ragweed (*Ambrosia* spp.), which shares the same habitat. Goldenrod pollen is too heavy to be carried by the wind; instead, it is carried by flying insects. • Each seed-like fruit is tipped with parachutes of white hairs. **Where found:** moist, open fields, woods and roadsides; throughout Ontario.

Pearly Everlasting

Anaphalis margaritacea

Height: 20–60 cm
Leaves: 3–10 cm long, hairy, edges rolled under
Flowers: disk flowers 6 mm across, yellow, enclosed by numerous white, papery phyllaries
Fruit: small achenes

The papery flower clusters of this hardy perennial grace roadsides for many months. They have a pleasant fragrance and keep their shape and colour when dried—excellent for dried flower arrangements. • This erect herb has white-woolly leaves (especially beneath). • Pussytoes (*Antennaria neglecta*) are similar, but have relatively large basal leaves and small (if any) upper stem leaves. **Where found:** open, moist to dry sites; throughout the southern ¾ of Ontario.

Common Yarrow

Achillea millefolium

Height: 10–80 cm
Leaves: 3–10 cm long, fern-like
Flowers: ray flowers white or pinkish; disk flowers creamy white; in heads 5–7 mm across
Fruit: flattened achenes

This hardy, aromatic perennial has served for thousands of years as a fumigant, insecticide and medicine. The Greek hero Achilles, for whom the genus was named, used it to heal his soldiers' wounds after battle. • Yarrow can be planted as an attractive ornamental, but beware—its extensive underground stems (rhizomes) can soon invade your garden. **Where found:** dry to moist, open sites; throughout Ontario.

Spotted Water-hemlock

Cicuta maculata

Height: 60–200 cm
Leaves: compound, leaflets 3–10 cm long
Flowers: small, greenish white, in flat-topped clusters 5–12 cm across
Fruit: seed-like schizocarps, 2–4 mm across

Spotted water-hemlock is one of the most poisonous plants in North America. All parts of the plant are poisonous, but most of the toxin is contained in the roots. This plant is easily confused with common water-parsnip (*Sium suave*), and a single bite can be fatal to humans. Children have been poisoned from using the hollow stems as peashooters. • Similar, introduced poison-hemlock (*Conium maculatum*) has purple-blotched stems and fern-like leaves. **Where found:** wet areas; throughout Ontario.

Common Cow-parsnip

Heracleum maximum

Height: 1–2.5 m
Leaves: compound, divided into 3 toothed leaflets, each 10–30 cm long
Flowers: small, white, in flat-topped clusters 10–20 cm across
Fruit: seed-like schizocarps, 0.7–1.2 cm across

This coarse perennial has large leaves, and flattened, egg- to heart-shaped, broadly winged, ribbed fruit. • The young, fleshy stems of cow-parsnip can be peeled and eaten raw or cooked, but do not confuse cow-parsnip with the deadly poisonous water-hemlocks (*Cicuta* spp.). • Many animals, including bears, eat cow-parsnip. **Where found:** throughout Ontario, but may be absent in northwestern regions.

Northern Bedstraw

Galium boreale

Height: 20–60 cm
Leaves: 2–6 cm long, narrow, in whorls of 4
Flowers: 4–7 mm across, white, in clusters
Fruit: paired nutlets, <1.5–2 mm across

Bedstraws are related to coffee, and their tiny, paired, short-hairy nutlets can be dried, roasted and ground as a coffee substitute. • Bedstraw juice or tea was applied to many skin problems. Some people take the tea to speed weight loss, but continual use irritates the mouth, and people with poor circulation or diabetes should not use it. • The flowers are arranged in repeatedly 3-forked clusters. • Sweet-scented bedstraw (*G. triflorum*) has broader, bristle-tipped leaves in whorls of 6, and its nutlets are covered with long, hooked bristles. **Where found:** open sites; southern ¾ of Ontario.

Curly Dock

Rumex crispus

Height: 50–150 cm
Leaves: 10–30 cm long, lance-shaped, wavy-edged
Flowers: greenish, about 4 mm long, in clusters 10–40 cm long
Fruit: papery achenes, 5 mm across

Curly dock is an edible plant with conspicuous flower clusters. • The leaves are a good source of protein, calcium, iron and vitamins A and C. Raw leaves may be bitter, but cooked leaves add a lemony zing to soups or stews. Dock leaves, like those of the closely related beet (*Beta vulgaris*), contain oxalic acid, which is safe in moderation but toxic if consumed in large quantities. • Traditionally, the seeds were removed from the hull and ground into flour or used as a coffee substitute. **Where found:** moist, often disturbed ground; southern ⅔ of Ontario.

Common Plantain

Plantago major

Height: up to 60 cm
Leaves: 5–18 cm long, basal, prominently veined
Flowers: tiny, greenish white, in narrow spikes 5–30 cm long
Fruit: capsules, 2–4 mm long

Since common plantain sprouts up on just about any disturbed ground, you've probably tried to rid this common weed from your lawn without realizing its uses. This nutritious plant is high in vitamins A, C and K and is said to taste like Swiss chard. The young leaves may be eaten raw but tough, mature leaves are best chopped fine and cooked. Plantain leaves may be steeped into a hair rinse to prevent dandruff. The strong veins of mature leaves were traditionally used as thread and fishing line. **Where found:** disturbed or cultivated ground; throughout Ontario.

English Plantain

Plantago lanceolata

Height: 15–60 cm
Leaves: 10–40 cm long, basal, lance-shaped
Flowers: small, greenish, in spikes 1.5–8 cm long
Fruit: capsules, 3–4 mm long

You may spot these weeds growing along roadsides, in gardens or in disturbed sites throughout much of North America. • Plantains are edible, and the young leaves can be used in salads or cooked as greens. The dried seeds may be ground into flour. Native peoples steeped the seeds and leaves into medicinal teas, used to treat upset stomach and sore throats. Heated plantain leaves were applied to cuts to disinfect them and reduce swelling. **Where found:** moist, disturbed ground; throughout Ontario. **Also known as:** ribwort.

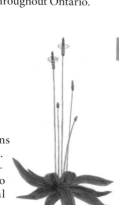

Common Reed Grass

Phragmites australis

Height: 1–3 m
Leaves: 20–40 cm long, 2–3 cm wide
Flowers: tiny, purple-brown, in a plumy panicle 10–40 cm long

Common reed grass is the predecessor of roasted marshmallows. The grass stem contains a sugar that was used in various ways. Some Native peoples converted the dried, ground stalks into a sugary flour that would bubble and brown like marshmallows when heated. Others shook the sugar crystals from dried stems or collected the sweet, gummy substance that bleeds from cut stems and ate it like candy. • The feathery, purplish flower clusters turn greyish as they mature to fruit. **Where found:** marshes, ditches and shores across boreal forest regions.

Wild Rice

Zizania aquatica

Height: 2–3 m
Leaves: about 1 m long, to 5 cm wide, toothed
Flowers: tiny, numerous, in spikes 60 cm tall and 30 cm wide
Fruit: grains, yellow to redddish

Wild rice grows mainly underwater and usually only the flowering head reaches above the surface. The yellowish to reddish grains were traditionally harvested by threshing the seed heads into a canoe. This edible grain is high in dietary fibre and protein, low in fat and a good source of several vitamins and minerals. **Where found:** shallow, still waters and pond edges; St. Lawrence River. **Also known as:** Canada rice, wild oats.

Common Cattail

Typha latifolia

Height: up to 3 m
Leaves: to 3 m long, 3 cm wide
Flowers: tiny, yellowish green, in dense spikes
Fruit: nutlets, 1 mm long

Tall cattails rim wetlands and line lakeshores or ditches across North America, providing cover for marsh wildlife species. They grow from long rhizomes that were traditionally eaten fresh in spring. Later in the season, the rhizomes were peeled and roasted or dried and ground into flour. • The flower spike is made of a cylindrical, dark brown female part topped with a spiky male part. The flower heads contain thousands of tiny, downy seeds. Fresh, dried seed heads were used to bandage burns and promote healing. • Narrow-leaved cattail (*T. angustifolia*) has leaves narrower than 13 mm and a gap between the male and female flower spike. **Where found:** marshes, ponds, ditches; southern ¾ of Ontario.

Bracken Fern

Pteridium aquilinum

Height: up to 1 m
Leaves: 90 cm long, triangular
Spore clusters: on undersides of leaves

Versatile, successful bracken ferns are found in almost every habitat except deserts and grow on every continent except Antarctica. • Bracken fern's 2–3-times divided, pinnate leaves form a triangle. Like other ferns, lines of brown spores cling to the undersides of the leaves. • Although Native peoples ate the fiddleheads and rhizomes, bracken ferns are carcinogenic to humans and animals and should be treated with caution. **Where found:** dry to moist forests, wetlands and roadsides.

Ostrich Fern

Matteuccia struthiopteris

Height: 0.5–1.5 m
Leaves: to 1.5 m long, 20–35 cm wide, tapered
Spore clusters: on shorter, fertile fronds 20–60 cm long

When you buy fiddleheads at the grocery store, you are most likely eating this fern. Ostrich ferns produce large fiddleheads that taste a little like asparagus and are rich in vitamins A and C. Only the coiled end is eaten, and no more than 3 fiddleheads per plant should be harvested, as picking more can kill the plant. • Ostrich ferns have ostrich-plume-shaped leaves that taper at both ends. The spores are found on the undersides of erect fronds that turn brown with age. **Where found:** wet to moist forests, wetlands, riparian areas and roadsides in boreal forest regions.

Common Horsetail

Equisetum arvense

Height: up to 50 cm tall
Leaves: small scales
Spore clusters: blue-tipped cones

Next time you come across a horsetail, feel the stem. Silica crystals cause the rough texture and strengthen the plant. Native peoples used the abrasive horsetails like sandpaper to smooth tools. • Most people are familiar with this plant's sterile "horse tail" stems that have many whorls of slender branches, but common horsetail also sprouts unbranched, fertile stems that are often overlooked. These smaller, brownish shoots have blunt cones at their tips and look similar to slender mushrooms. **Where found:** moist to wet forests, wetlands and disturbed sites; throughout Ontario.

GLOSSARY

A

achene: a seed-like fruit, e.g., sunflower seed

alcids: a family of birds that includes puffins, murrelets, auklets and other similar birds

algae: simple photosynthetic aquatic plants lacking true stems, roots, leaves and flowers, and ranging in size from single-celled forms to giant kelp

altricial: animals that are helpless at birth or hatching

ammocetes: larval lamprey

anadromous: fish that migrate from salt water to fresh water to spawn

annual: plants that live for only 1 year or growing season

anterior: situated at or toward the front

aquatic: water frequenting

arboreal: tree frequenting

autotrophic: an organism that produces its own food, e.g., by photosynthesis

B

barbels: fleshy, whisker-like appendages found on some fish

basal leaf: a leaf arising from the base of a plant

benthic: bottom feeding

berry: a fleshy fruit, usually with several to many seeds

bivalve: a group of molluscs in which the animal is enclosed by 2 valves (shells)

bract: a leaf-like structure arising from the base of a flower or inflorescence

bracteole: a small bract borne on a leaf stalk

brood parasite: a bird that parasitizes other bird's nests by laying its eggs and then abandoning them for the parasitized birds to raise, e.g., brown-headed cowbird

bulb: a fleshy underground organ with overlapping, swollen scales, e.g., an onion

C

calyx: a collective term for the sepals of a flower

cambium: inner layers of tissue that transport nutrients up and down the plant stalk or trunk

canopy: the fairly continuous cover provided by the branches and leaves of adjacent trees

capsules: a dry fruit that splits open to release seeds

carapace: a protective bony shell (e.g., of a turtle) or exoskeleton (e.g., of beetles)

carnivorous: feeding primarily on meat

carrion: decomposing animal matter; a carcass

catkin: a spike of small flowers

chelipeds: the clawed first pair of legs, e.g., on a crab

compound leaf: a leaf separated into 2 or more divisions called leaflets

cone: the fruit produced by a coniferous plant, composed of overlapping scales around a central axis

coniferous: cone-bearing; seed (female) and pollen (male) cones are borne on the same tree in different locations

corm: a swollen underground stem base used by some plants as an organ of propagation; resembles a bulb

crepuscular: active primarily at dusk and dawn

cryptic colouration: a colouration pattern designed to conceal an animal

D

deciduous: a tree whose leaves turn colour and are shed annually

defoliating: dropping of the leaves

disk flower: a small flower in the center, or disk, of a composite flower (e.g., aster, daisy or sunflower)

diurnal: active primarily during the day

dorsal: the top or back

drupe: a fleshy fruit with a stony pit, e.g., peach, cherry

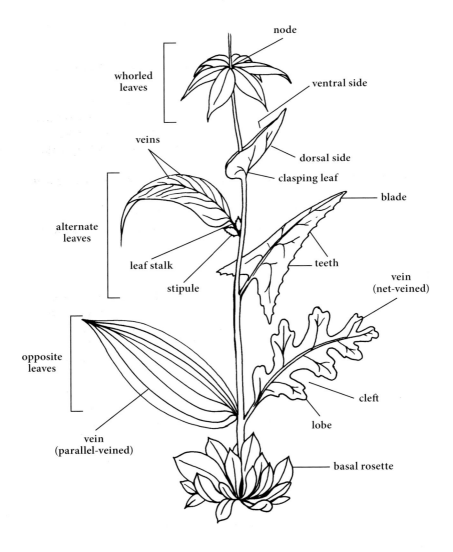

E

echolocation: navigation by rebounding sound waves off objects to target or avoid them

ecological niche: an ecological role filled by a species

ecoregion: distinction between regions based upon geology, climate, biodiversity, elevation and soil composition

ectoparasites: skin parasites

ectotherm: an animal that regulates its body temperature behaviourally from external sources of heat, i.e., from the sun

eft: the stage of a newt's life following the tadpole stage, in which it exits the water and leads a terrestrial life; when the newt matures to adulthood it returns to the water

endotherm: an animal that regulates its body temperature internally

estivate: a state of inactivity and a slowing of the metabolism to permit survival in extended periods of high temperatures and inadequate water supply

estuarine: an area where a freshwater river exits into the sea; the salinity of the seawater drops because it is diluted by the fresh water

eutrophic: a nutrient-rich body of water with an abundance of algae growth and a low level of dissolved oxygen

evergreen: having green leaves through winter; not deciduous

exoskeleton: a hard outer encasement that provides protection and points of attachment for muscles

F

flight membrane: the membrane between the fore and hind limbs of bats and some squirrels that allows bats to fly and squirrels to glide through the air

follicle: the structure in the skin from which hair or feathers grow; a dry fruit that splits open along a single line on one side when ripe; a cocoon

food web: the elaborated, interconnected feeding relationships of living organisms in an ecosystem

forb: a broad-leaved plant that lacks a permanent woody stem and loses its aboveground growth each year; may be annual, biennial or perennial

fry: a newly hatched fish that has used up its yolk sac and has commenced active feeding

G

gillrakers: long, thin, fleshy projections that protect delicate gill tissue from particles in the water

glandular: similar to or containing glands

H

habitat: the physical area in which an organism lives

hawking: feeding behaviour in which a bird leaves a perch, snatches its prey in midair, and then returns to its previous perch

herbaceous: feeding primarily on vegetation

hibernation: a state of decreased metabolism and body temperature and slowed heart and respiratory rates to permit survival during long periods of cold temperature and diminished food supply

hibernaculum: a shelter in which an animal, usually a mammal, reptile or insect, chooses to hibernate

hind: female elk (this term is used mostly in Asia—in North America "cow" is more often used)

hips: the berry-like fruit of some plants in the rose family (Rosaceae)

holdfast: the root-like structure that seaweeds use to hold onto rocky substrates

hybrids: the offspring from a cross between parents belonging to different varieties or subspecies, sometimes between different subspecies or genera

I

incubate: to keep eggs at a relatively constant temperature until they hatch

inflorescence: a cluster of flowers on a stalk; may be arranged as a spike, raceme, head, panicle, etc.

insectivorous: feeding primarily on insects

intertidal zone: the area between low- and high-tide lines

invertebrate: any animal lacking a backbone, e.g., worms, slugs, crayfish, shrimps

involucral bract: one of several bracts that form a whorl below a flower or flower cluster

irruptive species: a species that occasionally appears in large numbers outside its usual range

K

key: a winged fruit, usually of an ash or maple; also called a "samara"

L

larva: immature forms of an animal that differ from the adult

leaflet: a division of a compound leaf

lenticel: a slightly raised portion of bark where the cells are packed more loosely, allowing for gas exchange with the atmosphere

lobate: having each toe individually webbed

lobe: a projecting part of a leaf or flower, usually rounded

M

metabolic rate: the rate of chemical processes in an organism

metamorphosis: the developmental transformation of an animal from larval to sexually mature adult stage

midden: the pile of cone scales found on the territories of tree squirrels, usually under a favorite tree

molt: when an animal sheds old feathers, fur or skin, in order to replace them with new growth

montane: of mountainous regions

myccorhizal fungi: fungi that has a mutually beneficial relationship with the roots of some seed plants

N

neotropical migrant: a bird that nests in North America, but overwinters in the New World tropics

nocturnal: active primarily at night

node: a slightly enlarged section of a stem where leaves or branches originate

nudibranch: sea slug

nutlet: a small, hard, single-seeded fruit that remains closed

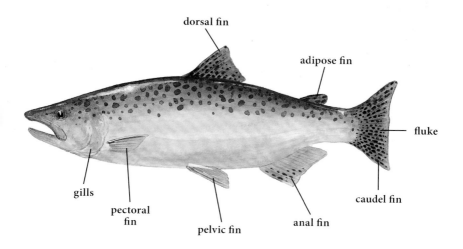

dorsal fin

adipose fin

fluke

gills

pectoral fin

pelvic fin

anal fin

caudel fin

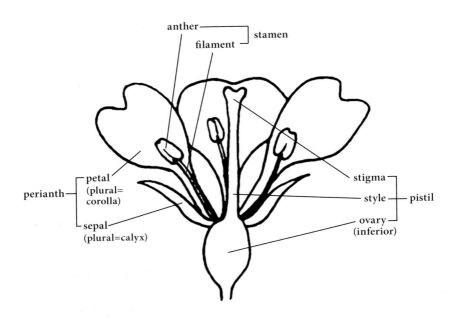

O

omnivorous: feeding on both plants and animals

ovoid: egg-shaped

P

palmate: leaflets, lobes or veins arranged around a single point, like the fingers on a hand (e.g., maple leaf)

pappus: the modified calyx of composite flowers (e.g., asters or daisies), consisting of awns, scales or bristles at the apex of the achene

parasite: a relationship between 2 species in which one benefits at the expense of the other

patagium: skin forming a flight membrane

pelage: the fur or hair of mammals

perennial: a plant that lives for several years

petal: a member of the inside ring of modified flower leaves, usually brightly coloured or white

phenology: stages of growth as influenced by climate

photosynthesis: conversion of CO_2 and water into sugars via energy of the sun

phyllary: a type of specialized bract found below the flower head in plants of the aster family (Asteracese)

pinniped: a marine mammal with limbs that are modified to form flippers; a seal, sea-lion or walrus

pioneer species: a plant species that is capable of colonizing an otherwise unvegetated area; one of the first species to take hold in a disturbed area

piscivorous: fish-eating

pishing: a noise made to attract birds

pistil: the female organ of a flower, usually consisting of an ovary, style and stigma

plastic species: a species that can adapt to a wide range of conditions

plastron: the lower part of a turtle or tortoise shell, which covers the abdomen

poikilothermic: having a body temperature that is the same as the external environment and varies with it

pollen: the tiny grains produced in a plant's anthers and which contain the male reproductive cells

pollen cone: male cone that produces pollen

polyandry: a mating strategy in which one female mates with several males

pome: a fruit with a core, e.g., apple

precocial: animals who are active and independent at birth or hatching

prehensile: able to grasp

proboscis: the elongated tubular and flexible mouthpart of many insects

R

ray flower: in a composite flower (e.g., aster, daisy or sunflower), a type of flower usually with long, colourful petals that collectively make up the outer ring of petals (the center of a composite flower is composed of disk flowers)

redd: spawing nest for fish

resinous: bearing resin, usually causing stickiness

rhinopores: tentacle-like sensory structures on the head of a nudibranch (sea slug)

rhizome: a horizontal underground stem

rictal bristles: hair-like feathers found on the faces of some birds

riparian: on the bank of a river or other watercourse

rookery: a colony of nests

runner: a slender stolon or prostrate stem that roots at the nodes or the tip

S

samara: a dry, winged fruit with usually only a single seed (e.g., maple or ash); also called a "key"

salmonid: a member of the Salmonidae family of fishes; includes trout, char, salmon, whitefish and grayling

schizocarp: a type of fruit that splits at maturity into 2 or more parts, each with a single seed

scutes: individual plates on a turtle's shell

seed cone: female cone that produces seeds

sepal: the outer, usually green, leaf-like structures that protect the flower bud and are located at the base of an open flower

silicle: a fruit of the mustard family (Brassicaceae) that is 2-celled and usually short, wide and often flat

silique: a long, thin fruit with many seeds; characteristic of some members of the mustard family (Brassicaceae)

sorus (pl. sori): a collection of sporangia under a fern frond; in some lichens and fungi, a structure that produces pores

spadix: a fleshy spike with many small flowers

spathe: a leaf-like sheath that surrounds a spadix

spur: a pointed projection

stamen: the pollen-bearing organ of a flower

stigma: a receptive tip in a flower that receives pollen

stolon: a long branch or stem that runs along the ground and often propagates more plants

subnivean: below the surface of the snow

substrate: the surface on which an organism grows; the material that makes up a streambed (e.g., sand or gravel)

suckering: a method of tree and shrub reproduction in which shoots arise from an underground stem

syrinx: a bird's vocal organ

T

taproot: the main, large root of a plant from which smaller roots arise, e.g., carrot

tendril: a slender, clasping or twining outgrowth from a stem or a leaf

tepal: a sepal or petal; used when both structures look very much alike and are not easily distinguished

terrestrial: land frequenting

torpor: a state of physical inactivity

tragus: a prominent structure of the outer ear of a bat

tubercule: a round nodule or warty outgrowth

tubular flower: a type of flower in which all or some of the petals are fused together at the base

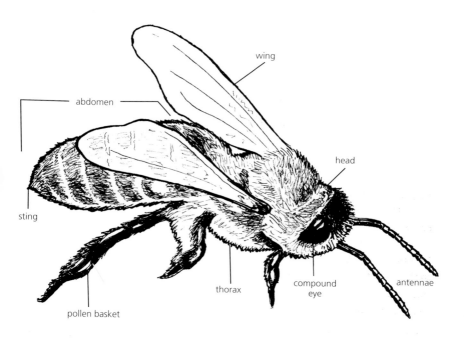

tundra: a high-altitude ecological zone at the northernmost limits of plant growth, where plants are reduced to shrubby or mat-like growth

tympanum: eardrum; the hearing organ of a frog

U

ungulate: an animal that has hooves

V

ventral: of or on the abdomen (belly)

vermiculations: wavy-patterned makings

vertebrate: an animal possessing a backbone

vibrissae: bristle-like feathers growing around the beak of birds to aid in catching insects

W

whorl: a circle of leaves or flowers around a stem

woolly: bearing long or matted hairs

REFERENCES

Acorn, John. 2007. *Ladybugs of Alberta: Finding the Spots and Connecting the Dots*. University of Alberta Press, Edmonton.

Acorn, John, and Ian Sheldon. 2003. *Bugs of Ontario*. Lone Pine Publishing. Edmonton.

Baicich, Paul J., and C.J.O. Harrison. 1997. *A Guide to the Nests, Eggs, and Nestlings of North American Birds*. 2nd ed. Natural World Academic Press, San Diego.

Behler, J.L., and F.W. King. 1994. *National Audubon Society Field Guide to North American Reptiles and Amphibians*. Revised ed. Alfred A. Knopf, New York.

Bezener, Andy. 2000. *Birds of Ontario*. Lone Pine Publishing, Edmonton.

Bird, C.D., G.J. Hilchie, N.G. Kondla, E.M. Pike, and F.A.H. Sperling. 1995. *Alberta Butterflies*. Provincial Museum of Alberta, Edmonton.

Boschung, H.T., Jr., J.D. Williams, D.W. Gotshall, D.K. Caldwell, M.C. Caldwell, C. Nehring, and J. Verner. 1997. *National Audubon Society Field Guide to North American Fishes, Whales and Dolphins*. Alfred A. Knopf, New York.

Dickinson, T., D. Metsger, J. Bull, and R. Dickinson. 2004. *The ROM Field Guide to Wildflowers of Ontario*. Royal Ontario Museum and McClelland and Stewart, Toronto.

Dobbyn, J. 1994. *Atlas of the Mammals of Ontario*. Federation of Ontario Naturalists. Don Mills.

Downs, W., P.B. Moy, L. Wiland, E. A. White, and S. Wittman. *Fish of the Great Lakes*. University of Wisconsin Sea Grant Institute. http:// www.seagrant.wisc.edu/greatlakesfish. Accessed July 2007.

Eder, Tamara. 2002. *Mammals of Ontario*. Lone Pine Publishing, Edmonton.

Ehrlich, Paul R., David Dobkin, and Darryl Wheye. 1988. *The Birder's Handbook: A Field Guide to the Natural History of North American Birds*. Simon and Schuster, New York.

Flora of North America Editorial Committee (eds.). 1993. *Flora of North America North of Mexico: Vol. 2. Pteridophytes and Gymnosperms*. Oxford University Press, New York.

Forsyth, A. 1999. *Mammals of North America*. Firefly Books, Buffalo, New York.

Forsyth, A. 1985. *Mammals of the Canadian Wild*. Camden House, East Camden, Ontario.

Great Lakes Fishery Commission. 2005. *Lake Ontario Fish Communities and Fisheries: 2004 Annual Report of the Lake Ontario Management Unit*. Prepared for the Lake Ontario Committee Meeting, March 29–30, 2005. Queen's Printer for Ontario, Toronto.

Hebert, P.D.N., 2002. *Canada's Aquatic Environment*. Revised ed. Cybernatural Software, University of Guelph. http://www.aquatic.uoguelph.ca/amphibians/. Accessed July 2007.

Hughes, Janice M. *The ROM Field Guide to Birds of Ontario.* Royal Ontario Museum and McClelland and Stewart, Toronto.

Kaufman, Kenn. 1996. *Lives of North American Birds.* Houghton Mifflin, New York.

Kershaw, Linda. 2002. *Ontario Wildflowers.* Lone Pine Publishing, Edmonton.

Kershaw, Linda. 2001. *Trees of Ontario.* Lone Pine Publishing, Edmonton.

Leary, B.P., and L.H. Leach. "Mapping the Potential Spread of Zebra Mussel (*Dreissena polymorpha*) in Ontario." *Canadian Journal of Fisheries and Aquatic Science* 49: 406–415.

MacCulloch, Ross D. 2002. *The ROM Field Guide to Amphibians and Reptiles of Ontario.* Royal Ontario Museum and McClelland and Stewart, Toronto.

Marles, R.C. Clavelle, L. Monteleone, N. Tays, and D. Burns. 2000. *Aboriginal Plant Use in Canada's Northwest Boreal Forest.* UBC Press, Vancouver.

Meades, Susan J. *Northern Ontario Plant Database.* http://www.northernontario-flora.ca/index.cfm. Accessed August 2007

Metts, Brian. 2004. *Animal Fact Sheets.* University of Georgia, Athens, GA. http://www.uga.edu/srel/animalfactsheets.htm. Accessed July 2007.

Newton, Blake. *Kentucky Critter Files.* University of Kentucky Department of Entomology. http://www.uky.edu/Agriculture/CritterFiles/casefile/casefile.htm. Accessed August 2007.

Roth, Sally. 1998. *Attracting Birds to Your Backyard.* Rodale Press, Emmaus, PA.

Royal Ontario Museum and the Ontario Ministry of Natural Resources. *Ontario's Biodiversity: Species at Risk.* http://www.rom.on.ca/ontario/index.php. Accessed July 2007.

Royal Ontario Museum and the Ontario Ministry of Natural Resources. *Ontario Biodiversity: Species at Risk.* http://www.rom.on.ca/ontario/. Accessed July 2007.

Runesson, U. *Borealforest.org.* Faculty of Forestry and the Forest Environment, Lakehead University, Thunder Bay. www.borealforest.org. Accessed August 2007.

Schneck, Marcus. 1999. *Garden Bird Facts.* Quantum Books, London, England.

Scott, W.B., and E.J. Crossman. 1998. *Freshwater Fishes of Canada.* Galt House, Oakville.

Sibley, David Allen. 2003. *The Sibley Field Guide to Birds of Eastern North America.* Alfred A. Knopf, New York.

Sibley, David Allen. 2001. *The Sibley Guide to Birds.* Alfred A. Knopf, New York.

Whitaker, J.O., Jr. 1996. *National Audubon Society Field Guide to North American Mammals.* Revised ed. Alfred A. Knopf, New York.

Wilson, D., and S. Ruff, editors. 1999. *The Smithsonian book of North American Mammals.* Smithsonian Institute and University of British Columbia Press, Vancouver/Toronto.

INDEX

Names in **boldface** type indicate primary species.

INDEX

INDEX

INDEX

ABOUT THE AUTHOR

Krista Kagume is a passionate writer of natural history and a born adventurer. She began birding at her family's cabin at the age of five. At age 17, she began a long solo voyage across Canada. En route she worked as a helicopter mechanic, a reporter for a weekly newspaper, a deckhand on a commercial fishing boat and a cycling tour guide. Eventually Krista earned a BSc in conservation biology and began writing articles on natural history for magazines and newspapers. She remains an avid cyclist and frequently heads off the beaten track in search of wildlife and plants.